Secrets to Lasting Love

UNCOVERING THE KEYS TO LIFE-LONG INTIMACY

GARY SMALLEY

A Fireside Book
Published by Simon & Schuster
New York   London   Toronto   Sydney   Singapore

FIRESIDE
Rockefeller Center
1230 Avenue of the Americas
New York, NY 10020

First Fireside Edition 2001
FIRESIDE and colophon are
registered trademarks of Simon & Schuster, Inc.
Manufactured in the United States of America

10 9 8 7 6 5 4 3 2 1

The Library of Congress has cataloged the Simon & Schuster
edition as follows:
Smalley, Gary.
Secrets to lasting love: uncovering the keys to life-long intimacy /
Gary Smalley.
p. cm.
1. Marriage—United States.   2. Communication in marriage—
United States.   3. Interpersonal relations—United States.
4. Intimacy (Psychology)   I. Title.
HQ734 S6855 2000
646.7'8—dc21   99-051622
ISBN 0-684-85050-8
      0-684-85051-6 (Pbk)

ACKNOWLEDGMENTS

This book represents the contributions of many people who are committed to help marriage grow to the deepest level of fulfillment. First, Jan Miller, my literary agent, who has taken this book on as if it were her own. Equal to that is Mark Seal, one of the best writers that I know of in the industry. Mark is professional and caring, which is hard to find in combination.

I would also like to highlight my two colleagues who work with me daily. They do research, write, and speak, and they happen to be my sons, Dr. Greg Smalley and Michael Smalley, M.A.

I want to thank the key professionals who have influenced my own research greatly, including Dr. Gary Oliver, Dr. Scott Stanley, Dr. John Gottman, Dr. Howard Markman, Dr. David Olsen, Dr. Susan Blumberg, and Dr. Dallas and Nancy Demmitt.

I want to express thanks to those who helped me discover the practical application to how these principles work daily. Thank you to Allison Slater, Sheri Thompson, Terry and Janna Brown, Jim and Suzette Brawner, Dr. Lee and Jane Orth, Todd and Angela Ellett, Allen and Janet Ritchie, Ed and Karen Akers, Joe and DebbieJo White, Derek and Pat McLean, and Jack and Sherry Heraschend.

To our staff at the Smalley Relationship Center who are dedicated and committed to enriching couples and families. They give tirelessly of their creativity and resources to help me learn what is truly helping couples today. Thank you. I could not do what I do without you.

Smalley Relationship Center Staff: Norma Smalley; Terry Brown; Jim Brawner; Dr. Greg Smalley; Michael Smalley, M.A.; Roger Gibson; Jimmy Funderburk; Lori Vanderpool; Sheila Smethers; Debbie Meyer; John Nettleton; Sheila Green; John and Marianne Webster.

CONTENTS

Secrets to Lasting Love

INTRODUCTION

What You Don't Know Can Hurt You!

IF YOU'RE THINKING, "Is there really a need for one more book on relationships?" you're about to be surprised. If you're wondering, "How could this book be any different from the hundreds of other relationship books already crowding the shelves?" you're about to get some invaluable proof. Because when it comes to relationships, what you don't know—and what you don't do—can hurt you.

What you might not know is this: Whether you're newly wed or "married forever," if you're not continually nurturing and deepening your relationship you may be lighting the fuse on a time bomb that can eventually blow, breaking your home, your family, and, finally, your heart. Lasting and loving relationships never have an "end"; they are either growing every day or stagnating.

You're living in the middle of a major revolution in the science of relationships. Of course, marriage researchers and counselors are always finding new and better ways to help the couples who turn to them for help. But the latest breakthroughs are something like the invention of the personal computer: easy-to-access technology that can not only render divorce obsolete but also take you and your mate into the deepest levels of intimacy. I've written sixteen books on relationships, but this new material has had a dramatic effect on my own marriage. My wife, Norma, and I have been married for almost thirty-six years, but we've dramatically improved our relationship over the past five years through the techniques you'll learn in this book. When I find something that improves the quality of my own marriage—something that has instantly helped hundreds of other couples—I want to share it, to spread it around. When I find techniques that can help lost couples find their ways back to happiness and contentment, I can't let those skills remain a secret.

Consider a couple I recently counseled. Len and Karen were caught in the all-too-typical cycle of heartbreak, making one last-ditch effort to save their marriage. They showed up at my office, having tried pretty much everything they thought was available to them. But then they were introduced to something that you're going to learn in this book: the three new powerful skills of relationship science. Within just one day, I could sense hope in their hearts and see their inherent love for each other lighting up their faces. After just two days, they fired their respective divorce lawyers.

What caused such a dramatic turnaround? What was the powerful "relationship antibiotic" that stopped all four of the "relationship germs" that were infecting their marriage? You read me right: we're talking about "germs." Len and Karen had been married for eight years—that number of years spoke volumes to me. The average life span of marriages in America is five to seven years before they fall victim to divorce. So they were right at the point of terminal stagnation.

But what they didn't know was ailing them.

They had met on a blind date. They hit it off immediately. Both professionals, they could afford an expensive courtship: they took exotic vacations, dined at the finest restaurants, and, before they knew it, found themselves madly in love and eager for marriage. It was almost like a natural reflex. "Why not tie the knot?" they thought. After all, they enjoyed many of the same things and activities.

There was nothing unusual about Len and Karen's courtship. Many couples meet, fall in love, and ride off into the proverbial sunset. But what they didn't know is that it's not just how much you love each other that makes a marriage; it's not how committed you are that will keep you together and in love for a lifetime; it's not the volume of your love. It's not even how well you try to "get along."

What matters most is how well you learn how to argue and nurture each other effectively. That's right! Argue. The four main causes of divorce, the "germs" that infect a couple, enter a relationship during ordinary, natural, everyday arguments.

Unfortunately, Len and Karen didn't know any of this—and what they didn't know was hurting them, big time. Eight years after saying, "I do," with two children, two cars, and an all-American household, they were about to fight it out in court. Instead of purring words of love, they would soon be barking epithets of hurt and pain: "No way, you're going to get that painting . . . You can't have the kids that long . . . Forget it, I won't agree to that"—on and on would resound the refrain of heartbreak. Why would people think they could "lovingly" argue in court when they never learned to argue at home?

Theirs was the same old sad story I hear over and over again. For the first four years of their marriage, Karen didn't share her true feelings of pain and despair with Len. She didn't want to "weaken" the marriage with continual complaints. That made perfect sense to her. Len wasn't able to "listen" because everything seemed fine to him, so they coasted into complacency. Then, after seven years, Karen began to complain about her loss of "loving feelings" for her husband. Len reacted to Karen by defending himself. He wanted Karen to "get counseling." Karen met his defenses with some of her own; she thought it was Len, not her, who should change. They argued constantly—without the insights of how to use disagreements to bring them closer together instead of driving them further apart. She wanted him to be more sensitive and more available to her and the kids. She begged him, "Give me more time to figure out what I want to do. I don't know why I've lost my feelings for you." He pressured her to make up her mind. He threatened to find someone else who could "really love" him.

The hurtful "infection" between them intensified and festered, until they found themselves in my office. I asked them if they had employed any relationship skills in their first eight years of marriage. Their answer was a resounding "NO!" I suggested that they try something new, to view their relationship from a different perspective. In less than twenty-four hours, I saw them attain a calm in each other's presence that they hadn't had for years.

Tearfully, Len looked at Karen. "We've had eight hard years," he said. "I'm willing to start all over again and do what we should have done in the first place. Are you?"

Karen looked hesitant, but she acknowledged that she, too, wanted to try. They were soon hugging, kissing, and talking about what they would do for the summer . . . not apart, but together. Where should they take the kids? Maybe they could redecorate the living room. Suddenly, they were planning a future together. In just a day, they had become a couple again.

It was yet another mini-marriage seminar, one more couple squaring off and sharing in a crowded room. But on this night, a major battle would be won and a lock to the doorway of the ultimate relationship would be opened, its wonders displayed for all to see.

The Journey Toward Intimacy

What did they learn? What was the power that transported this couple from the doorstep of divorce to a new world of understanding practically overnight? It's extremely simple. But what you don't know can, of course, seem extraordinarily complex. To put it simply, they learned that every relationship is a journey, not from birth to death, or from marriage to divorce. It's a journey through five levels of intimate communication, each level taking a couple deeper toward the naturally desired destination of the human heart: intimacy. They began learning and implementing three basic skills that could help them find deeper, lasting, and satisfying love.

In the transcendent moment of their reconciliation I saw a door open. When a man and a woman are able to lay down their emotional armor, when they can open their ears to each other and lay aside their individual positions, they will not only experience temporary reconciliation but also begin the journey to the place that each fully realized relationship is ideally headed: the journey toward intimacy.

How do you get there? You follow the "Map." This map is the essence of what you're going to learn in this book: *The ingrained relational knowledge that exists today can be read not as a static manual—not some dry, lifeless book on a shelf—but as a map, a dynamic road map, with directions, signs, and an ultimate destination that both a man and a woman can follow to an ultimate relationship.* To create this map, I've taken all my more than thirty years of marital research, resulting in a system that I believe is the clearest, most simple method I've ever developed. It can not only help you grasp the latest revolutionary relationship techniques but dramatically improve—or even save—your relationship in a matter of days.

This map has been a long time coming. In all of my years teaching and counseling couples about ultimate relationships, I really thought I knew how to help them. As I said, I've written sixteen best-selling books on the subject with titles like *Love Is a Decision* and *If Only He Knew: Understanding Your Wife.* I've been at the forefront of research in the current enlightened-relationship revolution; my videos, hosted by John Tesh and Connie Selleca, have sold millions of copies via one of the longest-running infomercials on television. I've become a recognizable face on network television, a regular on many TV talk shows. Recently, I have interviewed tens of thousands of men and women in seminars and surveys, on airplanes and in shopping malls, about what it takes to create a great relationship. In my individual counseling, I've been a one-man SWAT team of relationship therapy, the constantly on-call counselor for couples in, or in route to, trouble. My phone rings incessantly, sending me on endless emotional rescue sessions with clients ranging from celebrities to everyday Janes and Joes, all caught in the seemingly inescapable quicksand of problematic relationships.

But the current relationship revolution has forever changed my thinking—and my strategies for helping couples. Now, the doorway to deeper and more fulfilling relationships stands open to you. I would like to welcome you with a promise: By the end of this book you will be equipped with invaluable methods for delving into the five levels of intimate communication. You'll see how reaching the deepest levels of intimate communication will lead you to the most satisfying and lasting love you could imagine. You'll learn the three new and powerful relationship skills I recently discovered, and you will know, first-hand, the amazing effect they will have on your marriage. You can banish the four most common divorce patterns from your relationship and turn your arguments into opportunities for deeper intimacy and greater love.

Embracing the Relationship Revolution

You are probably wondering how three skills could so dramatically help you make your relationship work. The answer to satisfying and profound relationships lies in the last word of that sentence: *work*. Great relationships *do* require work. Most of us are willing to work hard if we know that our efforts will produce satisfying results, but often in relationships it is hard to see the end of such a steep road. We need help to understand what it is we are working toward.

Fortunately, these days, help is not only available for struggling couples, there is a veritable revolution underway, sweeping across America like a California wildfire caught in Santa Ana winds. Nothing like it has happened before in my lifetime. Already, more than 100 major cities have organized clergy, judges, and others responsible for performing marriage ceremonies to sign an agreement that they will not marry a couple unless the couple has received premarital training. It's an exciting time for the institution of marriage.

This new American revolution is a sort of backlash to the high divorce rate, the rising statistics of unhappy marriages, and the pain inflicted upon members of Generation X from their parents' all-too-frequent divorces. People are sick and tired of the marriage and divorce epidemic that's cutting down couples all over the world—and they are ready to do something about it! My research has convinced me that people recognize there must be a better way to live and to deal with the degree of unhappiness found within so many relationships.

Adding to the "marital wildfire" sweeping the land is the awareness of existing, scientifically tested marital training programs. These programs have been proving that marriages can be more satisfying and the divorce rate can be greatly reduced. There are at least twenty top programs available today, including PREP, the program headed by Drs. Howard Markman and Scott Stanley from Denver University. Drs. Markman and Stanley can predict divorce with over 90 percent accuracy, and their program can reduce divorce by as much as 50 percent. If every couple in America took their training, we might have only a 25 percent divorce rate in this country! Markman and Stanley even have a short test of eight questions that can predict how well a couple will fare for the future. Then there is Dr. David Olson, who has a outstanding pre- and postmarriage evaluation exam with 195 questions. This test is one of the best for predicting the outcome of a marriage even *before* the wedding day.

If you also consider the programs led by Drs. John and Julie Gottman, Harvel Hendricks, and Sherod Miller, as well as the work of Stephen Covey, you can see how much work is being done to improve the status quo of marriage and family in the beginning of the new millennium.

I am overwhelmingly convinced that if couples received instruction by using any of these programs, both before and after marriage, America could see the divorce rate significantly lowered within ten years. Imagine the possibilities: couples staying together with their children for thirty and forty years, kids growing up in loving and stable homes! It would be like heaving a massive boulder into the lake of divorce; the ripples of change would be limitless. Crime, teen prenancy, drug and alcohol abuse, spousal and family abuse, and so many other social maladies could be impacted for the better.

The possibilities are endless . . . but it all begins with two; *it begins with you!* Your future and the future of your relationship are up to you.

Directions on the Heart

In reading this book, you are embarking upon a pilgrimage to a most hallowed and sacred place: the realm of true and lasting intimacy. But this book is not just about the destination; it's about the *journey* to get there, a journey that begins, moves, and ends with the thread of intimate communication.

Before you begin the journey to intimacy, you must first realize why intimacy does not often occur naturally. The reason is simple: men and women are inherently different, even in their respective definitions of intimacy itself. For most men, intimacy is usually "doing activities with someone" even if they are not talking about feelings or needs. But the average woman says intimacy is usually "sharing verbally about experiences or feelings and needs." Place these two genders in the same house, call it a marriage, and what do we usually get? Two people trying desperately to fit into each other's mode and mind set. It's usually awkward, often painful, and frequently frustrating. Before long, the two can fall into relational patterns that lead them to divorce without them even knowing how it happened.

I'm always trying to find the ways to bridge these two distinct forces called "male" and "female."

Where do we begin? I believe the key is in understanding that men and women are very different in how they need to experience emotional intimacy. Of course, men and women are different in almost every emotional and mental aspect. So how can these almost different species stay together in a loving, satisfying marriage? One major step, a process we will discuss in this book, is to not just understand the inherent differences between the genders but also to bridge those differences.

Consider this example of a conversation I recently overheard: two women talking about a haircut.

WOMAN 1: *"Oh, you got a haircut! It's so cuuuuuute!"*
WOMAN 2: *"Do you think so? I wasn't sure when my stylist gave me the mirror. I mean, you don't think it's too fluffy looking?"*

WOMAN 1: *"Oh no, it's perfect! I'd love to get my hair cut like that but I think my face is too wide. I'm pretty much stuck with this style, I think."*

WOMAN 2: *"Are you serious? I think your face is adorable. And you could easily get one of those layer cuts—that would look so cute on you. I was actually going to do that except that I was afraid I would accent my long neck."*

WOMAN 1: *"Oh, now that's funny! I would love to have your neck! Anything to take attention away from this two-by-four I have for a shoulder line."*

WOMAN 2: *"Are YOU kidding? I know girls who would love to have your shoulders. Everything drapes so well on you. I mean, look at my arms, see how short they are? If I had your shoulders I could get clothes to fit me so much easier."*

WOMAN 1: *"Do you think so? Oh, you're just saying that!"*

WOMAN 2: *"No! Really, I mean it . . ."*

Now, consider two men discussing a haircut:

MAN 1: *"Got a haircut, didn't you?"*

MAN 2: *"Yep."*

Is this example of conversational differences the result of culture or genetics?

Certainly not every male and every female falls into these categories, but for thirty years I've seen similar characteristics in most couples. Men generally desire more independence. They are problem solvers more than they are listeners. They vigorously resist being controlled. Men tend to be turned on sexually by visual images and they are less influenced by emotional forces.

Women, on the other hand, generally possess deep desires for relational connections, a sense of community, and a desire for harmony.

Is it any wonder that men and women have different definitions of intimacy?

These differences are what can lead a couple down the path to an unsatisfying marriage. For women, it can be that they are often too critical of their spouses, too harsh when trying to begin a discussion with them, or overly sensitive and re-active to their feelings. Men can be too aloof, too independent (accusing their wives of trying to control them), too cold, and too objective. Men may try to lecture when trying to solve problems, when their wives only seek to be understood and heard.

Recently, while talking to two men about their relation-ships with their wives, one of the men told me a revealing story. He and his best friend like to rise before dawn and go jogging together. They have always enjoyed their runs and the companionship they share in them. But when he would return home, his wife would ask him about his jogging partner and his partner's family and what he and his jogging partner had discussed during their run. And he could never remember any of these details! The wife wanted to know the minutiae of how the other couple was doing, but her husband had trouble pro-ducing this information for her.

Finally, the man and his jogging partner decided that every morning, they would exchange a few facts with each other about their wives and kids, then memorize those facts so that they could "report" them to their wives when they got home. Neither man really cared about getting all the facts about the other's life and family; they just wanted to be able to get each of their wives off their backs. Once they had ex-changed the required facts, the two men would resume dis-cussing what they really wanted to talk about and they would enjoy their run.

This story strikes at the heart of some invaluable wisdom I've learned from women: most women know that meaningful communication is the essence of a loving marriage. I'm talking about something far deeper than just a superficial conversa-tion. While most women know that deep communication is crucial, many of them don't know how to get there with their husbands. They try and try and nothing seems to work. Still, *communication* is the starting point of the road map to inti-macy—and communication is the fuel that will take you to the desired destination.

Now, let's begin the journey. The place where you are heading is not easy to reach. It's going to take considerable courage and concentration to get there, but once you experience this wondrous place, you will never want to go back to where you were before. Because you are headed now into the place where the superficial subsides and love springs eternal, where you and your mate will experience true and lasting love.

CHAPTER ONE

Deeper: The Direction Toward the Ultimate Relationship

EVERY FULLY REALIZED RELATIONSHIP is a trip from surface emotions down into the depths, descending through five distinct levels of intimate communication that move from the shallow levels to the fifth and deepest level. At this fifth level, a couple feels absolutely safe and accepted for what they feel and need as unique individuals. Throughout this book I am going to show you how to accelerate your journey through these levels, arriving at the deepest level in the shortest, most effective amount of time. For now, let's discuss the five levels, so you'll understand what your journey is going to entail.

These five levels of intimate communication were first introduced in John Powell's book, *Why Am I Afraid to Tell You Who I Am?* But later, Dr. Gary Oliver, head of the Center for Marriage and Family at John Brown University, helped me understand that my entire life's work could be grouped within these five levels. All couples will move in and out of one or more of these five levels of intimate communication every day. This book will help you understand the five levels of intimate communication and how to use three powerful relationship skills to move in and out of all five levels anytime you wish. These levels are the outline of this book. Now I realize just how powerful they are:

The Five Levels
of Intimate Communication

1. Speaking in clichés
2. Sharing facts
3. Sharing opinions
4. Sharing feelings
5. Sharing needs

The first two levels are natural, easy, almost effortless. I've discovered that a majority of couples, sadly, can remain in these levels throughout their relationship.

THE FIVE LEVELS OF
INTIMATE COMMUNICATION

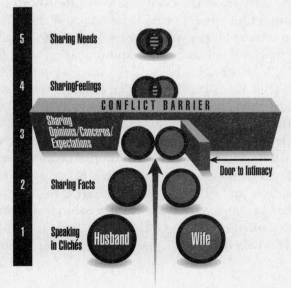

When you embark on a journey toward intimacy, in a sense you are "diving into" your relationship. Perhaps you and your mate have spent years climbing through the mountains, the ups and downs of your relationship. But now you've reached an awesome sight: the ocean. You don't want to remain stranded on the shore or stay stuck at the surface. You want to dive in deeply, to leave the shallow waters of superficiality and delve into, and revel in, the depths of intimacy. If you've ever experienced scuba diving, you know the feeling: it will be a long and frequently tough dive, but you will be amazed at the wonders you will find under the surface!

As you and your mate communicate with each other in the course of your daily routines, you are unconsciously always moving in and out of one of the five levels. Here is an explanation of each one:

LEVEL ONE: *Sharing clichés with each other.* This is surface talk, down only just below the water's surface, perhaps four or five feet. You're engaged in almost meaningless chatter. "Hey, how are you, how are you doing?" asks one spouse. "Okay, great, no problem," replies the other.

LEVEL TWO: *Sharing facts with each other.* You're talking about the weather, the office, what's going on with your friends. You're down deeper, but just barely, perhaps four or seven feet down. It's a safe level, requiring no deep breathing, thinking, or feeling.

LEVEL THREE: *Sharing opinions with each other.* This includes discussing individual opinions, concerns, and expectations, including personal goals, dreams, and desires. Now you're finally getting into the depths, and your initial reaction, as when scuba diving, is most likely fear. Your oxygen is dissipating and your ears are suffering the pressure. Sharing opinions is like diving to the eight- to fifteen-foot range; you may instinctively want to retreat to the shallower levels.

Most people can learn to dive down ten feet, pick up a seashell or two, and then retreat to the surface. But to reap the treasures in your relationships, you must learn to stay in the depths. As in diving, you must have the skills to give you the confidence to stay at this level—and also to go deeper. Nobody in his right mind begins a session in scuba diving without training. But couples all over the world begin relationships without even the slightest guidance, which is why they often remain at the shallowest levels of intimacy.

Speaking in clichés and sharing facts are safe harbors from conflict. But opinions are something else entirely. Opinions cause conflict, and conflict is extremely scary to most people. If a couple uses Level 3—the sharing of opinions—as a wrestling ring or a jousting court, if they're forever trying to "get" each other, to prove their respective views, concerns, and needs as superior to the other's, they're headed toward trouble. This type of slowly escalating jousting creates fertile soil for the seeds that can grow into divorce. But if each party attempts to refocus his or her thinking on trying to understand the mate, instead of trying to "convince" the other that a particular opinion is superior, then they can become a team.

That's usually easier said than done, because when couples move from Level 2 to Level 3, from sharing facts to sharing opinions, they hit a barrier: conflict. This conflict can be compared to a doorway that takes tremendous time and work to pass through before the couple can move down to Levels 4 and 5, which, in our scuba diving analogy, are the deepest and safest levels to which a couple can "dive."

But conflict can work two ways: Most often, it breaks couples apart. But it also delivers them to the deeper levels. Yes, conflict is the doorway to intimacy, but for most couples it remains an immovable roadblock. **Clichés are a cakewalk and facts are usually benign, but sharing opinions, concerns, and expectations? Opinions are the Pandora's box; they create conflict.** So one or both partners will tend to become "infected" with one or more of four main "relational germs"—withdrawal, escalation, belittling, or developing false beliefs about each other—and will never get to the deepest, most fulfilling levels. Most couples in conflict can't see that the very force that is battering them is essential to reaching a deeper

relationship. They're too busy with the struggle of daily existence to search for the depth beyond the conflict.

LEVEL FOUR: *Sharing your deepest and truest feelings with each
other.* At this level, you help each other feel safe to share your
deepest emotions. You each know that you will both do your
very best to listen and value what the other is sharing. Each of
you can accept the other as unique and special, a creation
made up of all your history, personality, and family background. It's as if each of you represents a different combination of "colors," and you can both treasure each other's
individual "color" combination. What's so exciting is this: as
you walk through the door of conflict to reach the deeper levels of intimacy, you are simultaneously eliminating all four of
the "divorce germs."

LEVEL FIVE: *Sharing your most important relational needs.* This
is the deepest level of love and marital satisfaction. You've been
together long enough and you feel safe enough to share your
deepest needs with one another. I have discovered from thousands of couples that seven needs keep surfacing as the most
important to both men and women. But the most intimate part
of loving communication is when both of you feel safe to reveal
your unique needs to one another. This shows that you know
you will be accepted and valued by your mate for who you are.

Guess how long it takes for the average individual to begin
sharing his or her feelings and needs? Six years. Again, the average time for divorce? Five and a half years. Why? Because
once you hit the third level of intimacy—sharing opinions—
you're at the greatest risk for conflict. Without some training,
you could stay conflicted at this level for some time. People
have an intuitive sense that danger lurks behind the door of
conflict. They don't realize that true love exists there, too. Most
people retreat from conflict, from the prospect of deeper levels
of intimacy, returning instead to the safer levels of sharing
clichés and facts, never breaking through, never becoming fulfilled, only becoming increasingly frustrated. Gradually, these

unaware couples creep into these four ineffective, destructive patterns, or "relational germs," leading to divorce.

They begin the "dance of conflict," the dance of disharmony, traveling among the three elementary levels, back and forth, back and forth, until their years of marriage take them no deeper—merely back to the superficial levels where they've already been. Fearing conflict, they play out the same year of marriage over and over again. They never get to the levels of fulfillment, Levels 4 and 5, because they're too busy doing the dance of conflict. I've known couples married for years, couples celebrating their twentieth anniversary. Each year, they do the dance of conflict all over again. Only the issues change— finances, vacations, retirement—the dance is always the same. They don't have twenty years of marriage, they have one year of marriage twenty times. Their relationship never deepens; it merely stretches forward in a straight, unemotional line.

Maybe you recognize yourself presently engaged in this dance of conflict. If not, you've certainly watched couples doing the dance—and it's not a pretty sight. Several years ago, my wife and I went on a vacation with a friend who absolutely will not allow his wife to discuss her feelings, much less her needs. That type of discussion is much too deep, too dangerous, especially for a vacation! He's in such control, in such denial, that he's even instituted a rule against discussions of these basic aspects of any relationship. His wife, forbidden to express her needs and feelings, has become a walking time bomb. The couple remains locked in what I call the rut of roles—a rut being a grave with both ends kicked out—each partner playing a designated part, acting out his or her life instead of truly experiencing it. She is eventually going to blow, taking whatever remains of that relationship. Remember the movie *Ordinary People*? Mary Tyler Moore played a character whose oldest son had died; she had one hard-and-fast unspoken rule: she spoke only in facts, never opinions, until eventually she imploded. Unable to share facts or opinions, she simply walked out on her family. Her fear of opening the door to reach the deeper levels was just too painful.

Avoiding conflict is far more dangerous than confronting it. Arguing is like starting a fire. You have to learn how to harness it properly, or it can tear you and your mate apart. Reaching these deepest levels of intimacy takes more than hard work and a willingness to delve deep; it takes a set of three simple, yet highly effective, skills that every successful relationship employs. These three skills represent my years of study, experience, and counseling and have revolutionized infinite relationships. If properly and consistently practiced, these skills have the ability to take your relationship to the deepest levels of intimacy.

Let's examine each of the three skills:

The Skill of Honoring

This is the lighthouse, the beacon, the mighty rock on which every fulfilling relationship is built and without which every shaky relationship is destroyed. When honor is present in a relationship, a couple can withstand the roughest storms. When honor has been destroyed in a relationship, the couple is destined for disaster. The best definition of honor that I've found is as any time we "confer distinction" upon someone. When a college bestows upon someone an honorary doctorate degree, the school is conferring distinction. When an audience applauds or an individual bows before someone, distinction is being conferred. Honor is not judgmental. Honor does not involve the belief that your opinions, concerns, and desires are somehow superior to your partner's. Honor does not involve getting your mate to see things your way.

Conveying a superior attitude is the biggest killer of marriage and produces the most frustration, hurt, and fear within a marriage. Honor is a "lifting up," a holding up of your mate with reverence. It's the selfless process of proclamation: in honoring you are telling your mate that he or she is paramount in your life and his or her status in your hierarchy of values is above all petty arguments, disagreements, and opinions. Honor is permanent, unmovable, forever. Therefore, the first act in cultivating honor in your relationship is to decide that your mate is worthy of honor; you must confer distinction upon that individual. This is the most important skill you can master; the others can't and won't work without honor. One

marriage expert says that without honor, all the other marriage skills won't work; another expert, Dr. Scott Stanley, has
said that honor is the fuel that keeps the lifelong marriage loving and functioning. If honor is nonexistent in one partner,
there is a high probability that the marriage is over. But if even
only a spark of respect or adoration remains, that spark can be
turned into a flame in a short time. I'll show you how to build
honor in your relationship, erecting a firewall to protect you
and your spouse from the flames that will certainly come.

Honor is the key that unlocks the door of conflict that
leads to deeper intimacy. It's also the physical act of grabbing
the knob and opening that door.

The Skill of Drive-Through Listening

This is the almighty skill of communication, an ingredient in
every fulfilling relationship. This skill allows you to take the
first few steps through the doorway of conflict down to the two
deepest levels of intimacy. I'm talking about the most powerful
communications skill known to mankind: drive-through listening. The method will allow you and your mate to feel listened to, understood, and validated, especially in times of
conflict. You've probably already practiced drive-through listening, whether you realized it or not. Every time you use a
drive-through window at McDonald's or Burger King, you've
engaged in drive-through listening. You place your order, then
the drive-through attendant repeats your order back to you.

Like the fast-food clerk who repeats the customer's order,
a mate using drive-through listening repeats what his or her
mate has said. This communication method not only clarifies
the conversation and prevents misunderstanding, it allows the
couple to discover the deeper meanings behind their words.
Just imagine how many millions of dollars these fast-food
restaurants have spent to find the best communication method
to stay "married" to their customers. We can use the same
method for free to stay married to our mates.

Constantly Recharging Your Mate's "Needs Battery" through Love

Human beings have an internal "needs battery," and our actions produce either positive or negative "charges" to our mate's battery. Loving attention given to each other's needs undoubtedly has a positive effect, while selfish, draining charges have a negative effect. It's been determined that couples literally throw hundreds of positive and negative charges at each other in a typical day of interaction. In Chapter 7, I'll share the top seven relationship needs with you and show you how to discover your own needs, as well as your mate's needs, so you can begin the process of meeting those needs and regularly recharging each other. The great thing about discovering the top needs of your mate is that it can help you understand conflict, as most arguments come from perceived unmet needs. That's right. Most arguments can be avoided if you care for the top needs of your mate. That's because surface arguments usually come from deeper unmet relational needs.

Dr. John Gottman, the father of many recent relationship breakthroughs, has shown that couples who divorce experience about ten minutes per day less "positive charge time" than couples who stay together but are unhappy. Gottman discovered that couples who stay together and are happy experience about ten more minutes of "turning towards each other" in positive ways each day than do the couples who remain married but are unhappy. In a similar way, I've discovered that if a couple spends a few minutes each day listening and understanding each other's feelings, it's like they are checking the state of each other's "needs" battery. Feelings are a gauge of how well needs are being met. Some feelings indicate a low battery, and include hurt, frustration, and fear; conversely, indications of a fully charged battery include joy, happiness, and ecstasy. The human needs battery should have daily recharging. How do you do it? First you have to discover what your mate's needs are.

These three skills may seem simple, but do not be deceived! Couples can't spend every moment in exercises and analysis.

The process of daily living tends to grind us down, pushing us to compromise, to accept instead of to choose what's best for our relationships. But there is always time for reevaluation and reawakening. And when you're talking about the most important union in your life, could there be any time but now?

Let me illustrate the power of these three intimate communication skills and the amazing changes they can bring about in your marriage by showing you how one couple used them. Jeff and Sarah came to my seminar in trouble. Their problems were nothing unusual—money, kids, minor sexual incompatibilities—but they could not work through them because they couldn't communicate with one another. When they came to my seminar, I asked Jeff to verbally give Sarah a questionnaire that would help them get past their communication barrier and allow their real problems to come to the surface.

The first question Jeff asked Sarah was, "What is one of the most important areas of our marriage that, if it were improved, would make our marriage much more satisfying?"

"Communication," Sarah answered firmly.

"What exactly do you mean by that?" he asked.

"I mean actually listening, not just nodding at me and saying, 'Uh huh, uh huh,'" she explained. Pain crept into her eyes. I knew, and I think Jeff did too, that he had immediately hit upon something important in Sarah's mind. It was the first skill, the skill of Honoring.

"What does 'listening' mean to you?" he asked.

"Well, I can see it in your eyes if you are actually paying attention and understanding what I am saying," Sarah said, "and then I know for certain that your walls haven't gone up."

Jeff paused for a moment. "So you're more concerned that I'm paying attention than that I'm listening?" he asked, trying to rephrase what she had said.

Sarah nodded.

"So you're trying to read my body's language to see if I am paying attention and understanding you, correct?" he queried further.

"Yes," she nodded again.

"Okay, then, what's in my body language that I need to improve to have you see that I understand you?" he asked, looking for a better alternative.

Sarah surprised her husband by having a very defined and immediate answer ready. "Stop smirking!" she exclaimed. "You laugh at everything. Everything is a big joke to you. Even when I'm being serious, you face me with this big grin on your face and I want to smack you!"

Wow. Underneath a placid, controlled exterior, Sarah was obviously harboring some big-time resentment. Here's a couple who, on the surface, seems fine, but once you delve below the surface—behind the mask or the smirk—they're actually in trouble. Behind the smirk and humor are pain and emotion. And that's where Jeff and Sarah had to begin their journey toward intimacy: to get behind what the smirk is masking and go deeper from there.

"I guess you don't understand that my smirking is a control mechanism; it's my way of saying let's not fight," Jeff said, as if thinking to himself out loud.

"That's true, I don't understand that," Sarah replied.

"What would it take to understand my smirking?" he asked her calmly.

"I don't know. You do it all the time. It's a continual thing for you. You do it at work, you do it at church, you do it at home, you do it with your kids." Sarah was trying to control her anger, but it was clear that this was a serious problem in their communications.

Jeff looked his wife right in the eye and, although he didn't realize it, began practicing the second skill: drive-through listening: "So, you're saying that one of your most important needs in our marriage is for me to act more seriously. My smirking is causing a communication problem?"

"Yes," Sarah confirmed. "I just don't think you take my concerns seriously enough."

"But I do take you and your concerns seriously," Jeff said, employing the third skill, recharging. "So what do I need to do to prove I'm more concerned?"

"Don't smirk! Don't laugh!" Sarah replied, and both of them began to laugh, in spite of themselves.

Jeff and Sarah had a huge hurdle to jump in their communications: misinterpreted behavior and a lack of mutual understanding. They eventually learned how to employ three powerful relationship skills that have the ability to take relationships deeper toward intimacy. They used the first skill—honoring—by showing their mutual interest in keeping the conversation going, instead of abandoning it as soon as things got rough. The second skill—a communications process called "drive-through listening"—was employed every time Jeff listened and repeated back to Sarah what he thought he was hearing, thereby clarifying and deepening the conversation. Jeff employed the third skill—recharging—by finding out what Sarah needed from him (being more connected through talking seriously, instead of facetiously). They immediately began to see the light at the end of their tunnel. They were able to explore intimate communication, and it led them back to each other's hearts.

These three skills are very powerful, yet I've discovered that most couples need only these three to propel themselves to the deeper levels. There are more skills in the relationship arena, but like most couples, you may find that you need only these to maintain a happy and fulfilling relationship. They are the foundation for ultimate relationships and your best defense against divorce.

Your Most Precious Possession

Now, maybe you're saying to yourself, "Intimacy? Who needs to go deeper? I'm happy where I am." But how would you feel if your spouse walked out? Think about this for a moment. It happens to people every day! If you're stuck in the shallow levels of intimacy—speaking in clichés or facts—you are also likely stuck in denial. If so, your partner may eventually hold up a mirror on your relationship, and you might not like what you see.

How important is your relationship? What would you give up to keep your mate?

Millard Fuller, the founder of Habitat for Humanity, gave

up everything—an opulent house in the nicest part of town, the Lincoln Continental in the driveway, the maid who cleaned the house and took care of his two children, two power boats, a vacation cabin, a huge farm stocked with cattle and horses, fishing lakes, and a substantial bank account—to win back his most precious possession: his wife's heart.

Fuller, a self-described "all-American, Alabama church-going boy," had spent his entire life trying to make money. "I was ambitious," he writes in his book *A Simple, Decent Place to Live.* "I wanted to make something of my life. And I knew the way to do it was to make money and lots of it—to be successful in the classic sense of the word."

As a developer and an entrepreneur, Fuller quickly amassed a fortune after his graduation from law school. He was soon worth millions. But along the way to wealth, he grew more and more distant from his wife, Linda, and their two children.

By age twenty-nine, he remembers, he was "totally consumed, totally focused; I had no concept of balance, and I certainly couldn't see past my lifelong goal. Linda, though, saw what I could not see—that our marriage also [suffered] from my incessant drive to make money."

They had been happy once—when they were just starting out, when they had nothing but each other—but that was ancient history. Because one day, his wife walked into his office and said a single sentence that made everything he'd accomplished seem petty and worthless.

"I don't think I love you anymore," Linda announced.

Fuller could barely believe his ears. After everything he had given his wife, he couldn't believe she could say such a thing.

"She told me that what I wasn't giving her was myself," he says. "She said she never saw me. She complained that the business was taking all of me." Fuller promised his wife he would change, and he meant to. But after another year, nothing had changed at all; Fuller still worked all the time and rarely saw his wife or their children.

Linda had finally had enough. She told her husband she was leaving him. She was considering a divorce and she

wanted time to think. She flew to New York and began counseling with a pastor there, leaving her shell-shocked husband
alone to ponder where their relationship had gone wrong.

"Ever since I was a teenager, I had always been in control
of things. Whatever I was involved in, I was the head of it," he
says. "It was the biggest shock of my life to realize that a decision was going to be made about our marriage—and it wasn't
going to be made by me."

Fuller had to do a lot of soul searching after Linda left. "I
realized I was about to lose that which was very, very precious
to me, which I had taken for granted. It was out of that crisis
that I had to start reevaluating what was happening in my life.
I realized I didn't want to lose my wife. I didn't want to lose my
family."

Fuller had to take care of the children by himself in
Linda's absence. "One evening as I was pulling the blanket
over my son, he looked up at me and said, 'Daddy, I'm glad
you're home.' . . . A chill traveled down my spine as I realized
that Linda was right. I had indeed become a virtual stranger in
my own house."

Millard Fuller is a persistent man. Aware of the mistakes
he had made, he kept phoning his wife until she agreed to see
him again. Linda's pastor had encouraged her to keep an open
mind, to remember that people can change, to give her husband the benefit of a chance. So she agreed to meet him—and
this is where the story gets interesting.

"I went to New York and I remember when I saw her: she
was staying at the Wellington Hotel and she looked so beautiful it just melted my heart," he remembers. "We talked and
ended up going to Radio City Music Hall. There was a funny
movie on called *Never Too Late*.

During the movie's intermission, Linda began crying. The
two decided to walk back to their hotel. "Somewhere off Fifth
Avenue, we opened up to each other," Fuller says. "Linda
spilled out all of the hurt and secrets that had built up as our
lives had grown apart. She cried as I had never seen her cry
before.

"We realized that we didn't want our marriage to end,"
Fuller said. "We got in a taxi and started back to the hotel, and

there was a real sensation of light in the taxi. It was not a spooky or mysterious type of thing. The only way I can describe it is a sensation of light. And in that moment, it just came to me that we should give away our money, that we should make ourselves poor again, the way we were when we first got married. I turned to her and said, 'I think we should leave the company, we should get rid of the Lincolns, get rid of the house, get rid of the cabin on the lake, get rid of everything. Give it all away and just start over.' She started crying. She was so happy. She felt like she was going to get her husband back."

The next morning, when they came out of the hotel and headed toward the airport, a new taxi glided up to the curb and the driver just sat there, beaming.

"Congratulations," said the taxi driver.

"For what?" asked Fuller.

"This is a brand new taxi," said the driver. "You're my first ride."

"We saw it as a sign from heaven that we had made the right decision the night before," said Fuller.

Back home, Fuller sold or gave away everything he owned—the trappings of success into which he had poured a decade of his life. Then, he and his wife embarked upon a wondrous journey, creating Habitat for Humanity, a nonprofit organization that has provided housing for infinite indigent individuals. Millard Fuller discovered something greater than money could buy: the wonders of a woman's heart.

So ask yourself: What price do you put on your relationship? If you are convinced that it is priceless—worth whatever it takes to nurture, strengthen, or even save—then you're reading the right book. Like Millard and Linda Fuller, you're about to embark upon a wondrous journey toward a place where you will receive a treasure more precious than gold.

The Journey Begins Now!

You've read what I believe are the bottom-line three basic skills—honor, drive-through listening and recharging your mate's needs through love—and you know your destination, the fourth and fifth levels of intimacy, on which both partners share feelings and meet each other's needs.

Now, let me show you how to become adept at each of the three skills, then we'll explore those levels, one by one.

CHAPTER TWO

"Are We in the Lowest Level of Intimacy?"

Clichés

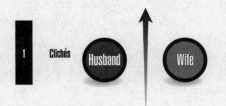

Cliché *1: a trite phrase or expression; also: the idea expressed by it   2: a hackneyed theme, characterization, or situation 3: something (as a menu item) that has become overly familiar or commonplace."*

—Webster's Tenth New Collegiate Dictionary

"A cliché is, in other words, a metaphor characterized by its overuse. I have my own test to see if a phrase is a cliché or not. I read the first half of a sentence, then I ask myself, 'Do I know (because everyone knows) how the sentence ends?"

—Internet posting

THE HONEYMOON IS OVER, the thank-you notes have been written, the wedding gifts are all unpacked, and you're using your new blender, Cuisinart, and china setting. But there's one gift that is usually omitted, a gift without which far too many couples go hurtling down an entirely different aisle from that of the chapel of love, straight toward heartbreak.

I'm talking about the gift of communication.

Each of the many women I've interviewed in my thirty-year career as a relationship therapist has listed communication as the most important tool in a successful marriage. Consider two excerpts from interviews with women in my seminars:

> *Through most of our marriage I feel that there has been a lack of communication. It's unfortunate that we really haven't taken classes on how to communicate with other individuals as we were growing up. It's such an important part of a marriage. But we are not really taught that.*

> *Communication is the area of my marriage that needs the most improvement. By that I mean actually listening, instead of just nodding and saying, "Uh-huh, uh-huh."*

The concerns of these women reflect that, for many couples, communicating can be a clumsy and frustrating process, sounding something like this:

> "How was your day, honey?" the wife asks.
> "Fine," the husband replies.
> "What happened at work?"
> "Work is work."
> "Are your clients being jerks?"
> "All my clients are jerks."

This couple, who we'll call Sandy and Dick, typify how most couples stuck at the shallowest levels of communication talk to one another. They use the official language of superficiality, the voices you heard on fifties TV sitcoms, the *Ozzie & Harriet, Leave it to Beaver, Father Knows Best* style of conversation that originates at the shallow end of the intimacy pool.

"We go through the same line of questions every night," Sandy says. "He never offers any personal information or insights, so we never get to the bottom of anything. He won't let me into his world."

The couple turns on the television set while they eat

dinner together, and their communication stops. "We don't talk while the TV is on," she says. So the TV is the only thing that speaks until it is time for bed. Then, the isolation escalates. "He reads his books, and I look through catalogs," she says. "When he is ready to go to sleep, he puts on headphones so he can listen to music until he drifts off, and I keep watching TV."

When they're forced into situations that require communication—like long drives—they resort to cliché speak: "We talk about the cats, the kids, our granddaughter . . . anything but us," Sandy says. "We talk a lot about our cats. The cats are safe. We bond through talking about our cats. We can't judge each other on anything we say about them. We can just sort of relax. I try to always be upbeat and positive. Sometimes, I feel like I am going to go crazy because we never talk about us. . . . We never say anything meaningful."

Sandy knows she and her husband have a problem, but Dick has erected a wall between them, a wall she dares not climb over for fear of his reaction. She's tried to discuss their lack of intimacy with him, "but he gets mad at me for bringing it up," she says. "He says that he will get there when he's ready. But in the meantime I'm going crazy. I feel like we are getting no closer, making no headway, and the months and years are rolling by."

And so they continue: together but apart, and going nowhere fast. But the ultimate relationship roadmap is always there. You can see it in a woman's natural inclination to move beyond the superficial levels of intimacy. If their husbands won't go to the deepest levels—sharing feelings and needs— they'll find somebody who will. I'm not necessarily talking about an affair, although we all know that can certainly happen. I'm talking about women getting on the phone with their friends and immediately going to the deepest levels. I'm talking about mothers immediately going to the deepest levels with their best friends, sisters, or daughters. Men have the same ability to go to the deepest levels, but I've discovered that, in many cases, it's easier for them to go to these levels with their friends instead of their mates.

For the husband left behind in the shallows—where he

will be eventually engulfed by swells—I have one question: "Wouldn't you rather she go to the deepest levels with you?"

Stuck Behind the Wall

Before you can get to where you want to go in your relationship, you have to first understand where you might most likely be stalled: in the shallowest level of intimacy, speaking in clichés with your mate.

If you're stuck speaking in clichés, it's probably not because you don't want to go deeper. It's likely that you just don't know how. Everyone has a strong basic need for intimacy. But most couples expect intimacy to happen automatically in marriage. They don't think they have to "work" at it. They believe that the act of being together will deliver them to the deepest levels of love.

You surely yearn to share your opinions, feelings, and deepest needs, to be understood and listened to and valued. But when you share your opinions, concerns, and expectations with your husband or wife, he or she—having natural differences—may disagree or react adversely or become silent or argue or try to convince you that he or she is right and you are wrong.

So you begin an insidious cycle. You want to get to the deeper levels of intimacy, but every time you progress to sharing opinions, whenever you get "real" with each other, you hit what feels like a wall—and, believe me, it is. It's a wall of conflict. There is a door through this wall of conflict, but you can't see it. So a seemingly innocent conversation explodes in conflict, critical remarks, condescension, and, eventually, retreat. Because, for most people, conflict is to be avoided at all costs.

As we discussed in Chapter 1, conflict is the very key to unlocking the doors of deeper intimacy. But when you're banging your head against the wall of conflict, it's painful. So you don't keep banging; you're eventually going to retreat and begin the dance of conflict. Now, let me show you how it works.

The music for the dance of conflict is our differences. Differences in opinions, differences in philosophies, differences in upbringing. Differences are inherent whenever two people

THE FIVE LEVELS OF INTIMACY

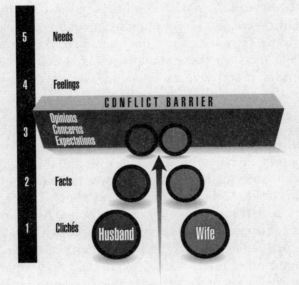

get together. "When you pick somebody to marry, you automatically have chosen your set of unresolvable relationship problems," says relationship expert Dr. John Gottman. "The couples that do well adapt to a problem and even have some amusement about it. The couples who don't do well get gridlocked and keep hurting each other's feelings and feel unaccepted and neglected when they talk about problems."

So with your differences providing the tune, you begin a predictable procession:

STEP 1: Critical remarks. One critical remark begins the dance. Unable to reconcile differences, one partner (or both) berates the other—"Look what you did!" "Why are you so impractical?" "Look how much you spent!"—and the journey toward intimacy ends and the verbal jousting begins.

STEP 2: Condescending comments. This escalates the tension of the critical remarks—and, believe me, this step hurts. Bam, bam, bam! The words land like blows. "Why can't you ever do anything right?" "Why can't you ever be on time?" "You're just like your mother/father/sister/brother!"

STEP 3: Return to safer levels. Conflict is painful, so one partner—or both—abdicates, retreating from conflict, returning to the safer levels of superficiality, once again speaking in clichés and sharing facts. At these shallow levels, a couple can languish for days, months, years, or decades before the dance begins anew.

This dance is occurring right now in infinite households around the world, a dance that is the absolute dirge of loving relationships. Couples are repeating this cycle over and over again, one mate growing increasingly frustrated over the other's inability to share his or her feelings or understand what is happening in the other's heart, while the other mate is oblivious to how desperate his or her situation has become. How does it usually end? With one mate's bags packed and his or her heart set on leaving, while the other is left asking, "What did I do wrong?"

But this event is preceded, as it always is, by an unspoken truce more eerie and perilous than the sound of any argument, a level of intimacy that is the equivalent of a long, deep sleep: speaking in clichés.

The Language of Limbo

Let's take a moment to analyze the language of the cliché level of conversation. No meaningful exchange of information occurs, only niceties and courtesies—all subconsciously designed to project an illusion of contentment. Of course, eventually the hidden frustration and suppressed feelings turn into despair and shatter the illusion. You find yourself going through the motions of marriage day after day, never getting deeper, until the very foundations of your relationship crumble.

Just as a lack of communication drives people apart, empowered communication skills have the ability to bring them together again. You must learn how to stop speaking in clichés and develop your relationship through communication. I'm going to show you how.

When I encounter a couple stuck in clichés—and it's more common than not—what I usually find is two people ignoring or denying the ultimate relationship roadmap. If a woman is stuck in cliché-speak with an unresponsive husband, she is either in denial of her intuitive knowledge or daunted by having to take on the responsibility of embarking on the journey to intimacy alone. Simultaneoulsy, many husbands don't realize that they are caught up in the cycle of clichés—so they have no way out.

If husbands and wives could instantly read the ultimate relationship roadmap, they would recognize clichés for what they are: obvious signs of a relationship stalled at the starting gate.

Escaping the Rut of Roles!

"I believe fact-to-face communication is very important. If it makes sense to marry at all, it makes sense to put ourselves in a position to talk. With you I have the feeling that we could go on and on, down ever-widening and branching and illuminating corridors, indefinitely or to an end that we don't yet imagine but which will have been worth it. Only with you do I have the feeling of interests opening up, rather than just playing out what I have already mastered. All is not, of course, marriage per se. But it would be our marriage, and I'm itching to get going."

"What do you think about now that you're married?" I asked Zelda.

"Well, we talk about who buys the orange juice and who makes the bed . . ."

—Married People, *by Francine Klagsbrun*

It's sad but true: far too many couples never get past the shallowest end of the intimacy pool: the level of speaking in clichés. As the quotation above painfully illustrates, it's usually the woman who has the longing for the journey down "ever-widening and branching and illuminating corridors," but instead find themselves discussing nothing deeper than buying orange juice and making beds. How can you escape the cliché stage? The first step is realization that the level exists and identifying yourself if you're caught inside of it. The second step is realization of how you ended up there.

Consider how clichés destroyed one well-intentioned couple. I ran across them in a beautiful book called *Living Happily Ever After* by David Collier, which tells the stories of a host of long-married couples. One couple profiled was Mort and Leslie Gerson. In their sixties, they've been together for forty years, first married, then separated, and now married again. What brought them eventual fulfillment? They were able to identify the cliché barrier and, after more than a decade of being caught in it, break through to a deeper, more satisfying level of communication and intimacy.

They "met cute," as they say in the movies, at a New Year's Eve party, when Mort left his date and pulled Leslie from her partner and tried to kiss her at the stroke of midnight. She thought he was "crude, crass, and presumptive," but she was somehow drawn to him. Leslie was buoyed by the adventure of romance, without taking time to analyze her feelings.

"I was hooked, but I wasn't like the Generation X of today, analyzing and saying, 'I want someone with the same spiritual, moral, and political values,' " she said in the book.

"Leslie was game for just about everything," Mort said. "It was an adventure."

So Leslie and Mort married, certain that the marriage ceremony, the simple act of saying, "I do," would transform both of them into perfect life partners. Before long, Mort had a high-stress job and Leslie had three children to care for at home. Without realizing it, the Gersons had begun the dance: two people moving increasingly apart as they fell into the rut of marital roles.

"Reality set in," Leslie said. "I didn't have a clue as to what raising children was all about. . . . Mort was so into his work that I had the whole responsibility of child rearing, and I felt very alone. I think our marriage problems started that first year, but I kept rationalizing."

They were stuck in the most common cliché of all: the rut of roles. Not only were they stuck speaking in clichés to bridge the widening gap between their worlds but also they were actually living a cliché. Leslie assumed the cliché of the homemaker and caregiver ("This is what marriage is like. Daddy goes off to work and mommy stays home with the kids," she says); Mort took on the cliché of the bread-winning husband.

When the breadwinner got home, he and his wife most likely spoke in the language of limbo.

> "How was your day, dear?"
> "Oh, fine."
> "Are you ready for dinner?"
> "Sure, dear."

And the TV remote control clicked off the seconds until bedtime.

For the Gersons, this was not acceptable. Leslie began wanting more. She'd phone her husband's office, complaining about something that was happening at home. But Mort was too deeply immersed in his role as provider to really hear her. Leslie was speaking on one level—about household problems—but really addressing a deeper level, her husband's unavailability and emotional distance. She felt abandoned and, eventually, angry. "During the first ten years of the marriage I had tried to be vocal about what was going on with me, but I was still extremely frustrated and resentful," Leslie said. "I remember wanting to go to a marriage counselor, but Mort would say, 'You're the one who's unhappy, you go, I'm not having a problem.' . . . I felt very alone and angry at Mort's inability to hear me on an emotional level and help me cope with the kids and the frustrations. There was a lot of confusion for us, and total unpreparedness for family life."

They never had the slightest idea that they were stuck in the shallowest and least satisfying level of intimate communication. But Leslie felt the yearning for more. She desperately desired a man she "could really communicate with, who would listen and understand and with whom I wouldn't feel ashamed to say anything to, and Mort didn't get that," she remembers.

So she left. She took their youngest child and left her husband in the home that he had emotionally already vacated himself. Like so many other people who are "the last to know," Mort could finally see his marriage as the cliché it had become: Leslie's decision to leave him was the last resort, but it was the only way to demonstrate to him how disconnected their lives had become.

Mort finally got the message that Leslie had been trying to send him.

"I realized I'd better tune in if I wanted to have a marriage, and I made a commitment to take a better look at who Leslie was and what was happening," Mort remembered.

They began seeing each other again, but Leslie remained cautious. "We were very careful with each other and worked on our relationship when we weren't married, and I was afraid that if we remarried things would go back to the way they had been," said Leslie.

Something remarkable happened while the Gersons were working on their "marriage-under-construction." Mort became more emotionally available. When Leslie phoned him at the office and said, "I really need to talk to you," he'd drop what he was doing and *really* listen. He had learned from their breakup that what Leslie was expressing was integral to their marriage's success. He had to transcend what he had formerly believed was his "role" in the marriage. He had to learn that he was a husband even when he was at work, and to respond to Leslie's needs twenty-four hours a day.

Leslie learned something important, too. "I hear so many people say, 'Well I thought marrying him would change him,' or, 'I thought he would change if I loved him.' With all the psychology and knowledge available, people still want to believe that something magic happens when you marry and that everything will be wonderful. That was me thirty-eight years ago. Now I realize that successful relationships are very hard-working, on-going struggles, where people learn to compromise and give and take and give and take." But most of all they learn to communicate at a deeper emotional level.

The rut of roles feeds clichés. Breaking through your role—as husband, wife, mother, father, provider—is a pivotal step in moving further toward deepest intimacy, ensuring a happier and far more profound relationship.

Rx for Cliché Speak: Embrace the Relationship Revolution

What could have saved the couple we've just encountered decades of heartbreak? What could have allowed them to take their relationship deeper, instead of merely further? What could have helped them to enjoy decades of marital support, instead of enduring decades of marital suffering?

The simple act of looking out from the rut of roles and discovering where on the relational ladder they rank.

I recently had an illuminating conversation with a physician in my hometown. He told me that over a century ago, an inordinate number of patients were dying on, or shortly after leaving, the operating table. Many lives were lost until a simple, yet pivotal, decision was made: the patients were dying from infection from nonsterilized operating instruments! The simple process of sterilization saved literally hundreds of thousands of lives. What was once a cataclysmic breakthrough has become elementary medical procedure. That's the way breakthroughs work: once you turn the light on, it's hard to believe you ever spent time in the darkness.

Similarly startling revelations are happening today in the marriage and family field. The centuries of standing by and helplessly watching the casualties, the bloodletting of those on the battlefield of relationships is over. The infections that cause the myriad diseases in relationship can be spotted early and, in many cases, cured. But just as we're learning what breaks couples apart, we're also realizing what causes couples to be happy, satisfied, fulfilled. That, to me, is the biggest breakthrough. Because while relationships have long been the most unpredictable of sciences, recent developments have allowed us to understand, and grow, relational intelligence as easily as you grow educational intelligence in school.

So what's the best way to break away from clichéd conversations and clichéd relationships? Embrace the relationship revolution. Start by asking yourself a few key questions. If you're ready to make the journey to the deepest levels of intimacy, then your starting point doesn't really matter. But before you can move downward, you should know how deep you still need to go. You have to discover your RQ. You probably know your intelligence quotient, your IQ. But do you know your relational quotient? Your RQ? If you think everybody is equipped with the same amount of relational awareness and skills, consider these excerpts from two very different letters:

> *My dear, lots and lots of love and please keep on loving me as hard as ever. You know I just feel as if a large part of me has been gone for the last ten days. P.S. There isn't anybody else on earth I'd stop to write at this time of day.*

> *Dear Gary . . . We have three children (9-5-2) and I was basically raising them on my own. I spent the majority of my marriage (9 years) feeling my husband must not really love me. But believing he did when the times were good. I finally couldn't stand it any more and asked him numerous times to leave. He was destroying his life with alcohol and depression and taking me under, too! I prayed God would let him hit a low or separate us.*

The difference is immediately clear. The first letter shows a natural aptitude for relationships. You can hear the writer's empathy and sense of caring and see his obvious skill for expressing it. The second letter illustrates an immediate need to grow and face emotions. The author of the first letter is none other than President Harry Truman, who wrote 1,300 love letters to his wife, Bess, during their sixty-year courtship and marriage. The second letter is from a student from one of my

seminars. Merely from reading the letters, we can see that President Truman was obviously in touch with his feelings, and,
even more importantly, the feelings of his wife, Bess. The second letter, however, reveals someone suffering under the yoke
of a husband who is not in touch with his feelings at all. President Truman exhibits optimum relational awareness, or RQ,
while the husband addressed in letter 2 suffers from a severely
deficient, if any, sense of relational well-being. RQs, like IQs,
are individualized. They are not "one size fits all." However, a
person's RQ can be characterized as high, average, and low.

Let me offer a few examples of couples displaying the various degrees of RQ:

• *RQ is not merely a function of intellect, but also of passion.* Consider a famous couple with very high RQ: What
about the original star-crossed lovers, Shakespeare's Romeo
and Juliet? These two Italian teenagers knew exactly how they
felt about their relationship, and they expressed their emotions openly and fervently to one another. It was only when
less RQ-empowered outsiders tried to interrupt their union
that the two met their tragic fates.

• *Individuals with average RQs merely exist instead of
thrive:* Probably the most famous American icon of Mom and
Dad, Ward and June Cleaver from the popular TV series *Leave
It to Beaver,* were as average in their respective RQs as they
were in every other respect. Wrapped up in their children and
their routines, both members of this couple seemed to coast by
in their relationship without a personal crisis or epiphany.
Their lack of passion with each other was in direct proportion
to their lack of confrontation. They were together in spirit, but
not in soul. They were absolutely ordinary and their relationship was a level line of complacency.

• *Individuals with low RQ are usually at war with each
other and their emotions:* No one would confuse the Cleav-
ers with another American TV couple who became stars
of pop culture just twenty years later, Archie and Edith Bun-

ker, the poster couple of low RQ in the 1970s. While Edith whined and flustered, often alone, Archie bellowed and grunted about, unwilling to be bothered with his wife's—or anyone else's—opinions. The two did have rare emotional moments, but mostly they seemed to always be battling life and themselves.

These are examples of couples with similar RQs. However, many couples are two people with very different RQs, and those marriages can often be the more distressed because of the discrepancy. When one partner has a high RQ and knows exactly how he or she feels and how to express his or her feelings, he or she will find it tougher to enlighten a low-RQ person, someone afraid of his or her feelings and unable to cope. We'll discuss how to help raise your partner's RQ later in the book. I'm going to show you how you can develop and raise your RQ as methodically as you develop your IQ—and it won't cost you any tuition, except for your time and attention. Mostly from what I learned from marriage experts and in helping thousands of couples around the world, I recently developed an RQ questionnaire for men and women, which you will find on page 57. Please take time to gauge your RQ, then set it aside until you've completed the book. After you finish the book, gauge your RQ again. I think you'll be surprised at how much you can learn and grow in the space of this book.

Breaking out of the Cliché Cycle

Your RQ shows you your starting point on the scale of relationship skills. If you're on the lower end of the scale, your first mission should be to break out of the cliché cycle. You've completed the first step by identifying yourself as someone whose relationship is stuck in the cliché level of intimacy. Your mission now is to identify and take the steps—no matter how small at first—that can deliver you to the next level of the journey.

I've developed a three-part technique in breaking the cliché cycle.

Relational Quotient Test

Review each question and mark the number that best describes your honest answers. When complete, total your score at the bottom and see what category you fall into. 1—Never   2—Seldom   3—Occasionally   4—Frequently   5—Very Frequently

____ I seek to learn what communicates love to my mate.
____ I initiate conversation with my spouse every day concerning the plans of the day.
____ I plan special dates so we can spend time together.
____ I initiate conversation with my spouse every day concerning areas where I am upset or angry concerning my feelings.
____ I initiate conversation with my spouse every day concerning how his/her day is going or has gone.
____ I listen to my spouse about all areas of his/her life.
____ I initiate discussion about conflicts that are unresolved.
____ I initiate discussion over sensitive areas that seem to be difficult to discuss.
____ I am open with my spouse concerning fears that I have in my life.
____ I initiate discussion concerning my mate's life dreams.
____ I enjoy listening to my spouse about all areas of his/her life.
____ I initiate reminiscing about our honeymoon.
____ I am open with my spouse concerning secrets about my past.
____ I initiate conversation with my spouse every day concerning my feelings about my day.
____ I am honest about disagreements over my spouse's opinions.
____ I tell my spouse how grateful I am when he/she meets my needs.
____ I compliment my spouse when he/she completes tasks for me.
____ I appreciate my spouse by giving special cards or letters to him/her.
____ I plan vacations so that we can become closer in our relationship.
____ I am open with my spouse concerning worries that I have in my life.
____ I appreciate my spouse by enjoying holidays together.
____ I show understanding when my spouse is angry with me.
____ I appreciate my spouse by taking time to plan events together.
____ I admire my spouse for his/her character.
____ I tell my spouse that I love him/her.
____ I enjoy listening to my spouse talk about what he/she wants out of life.
____ I laugh together with my spouse.
____ I reminisce with my spouse about our date experiences before marriage.
____ I initiate reminiscing about our wedding.
____ I show understanding when my spouse is discouraged.

(continue with next column)

____ I plan events and activities where we can have fun and play together (without kids).
____ I initiate reminiscing about special experiences that have drawn us together.
____ I plan events and parties so we can be with other couples.
____ My angry outbursts negatively affect our relationship.
____ During arguments with my mate, I am able to control my anger and frustration.
____ I avoid put-downs or other negative statements in our relationship.
____ I look for nonverbal signs of worry in my spouse.
____ I know what communicates love to my mate.
____ I look for nonverbal signs of frustration in my spouse.
____ I am sensitive when my spouse is hurt.
____ My spouse feels I care or am sensitive when he/she is hurting.
____ I know what I need from my spouse in terms of affection.
____ I communicate honestly with my spouse concerning my needs for affection.
____ I physically exercise with my mate.
____ I plan recreational events that we can do together.
____ I initiate holding hands with my spouse.
____ I initiate taking walks with my mate.
____ I give back rubs to my spouse.
____ I caress my spouse in a romantic setting.
____ I give my spouse romantic hugs.
____ I am affectionate without it leading to sex.
____ I describe my feelings of affection for my spouse regularly.
____ I express my passion for my spouse.
____ I ask my mate what kind of affection he/she enjoys.
____ I kiss my spouse to show my affection.
____ I encourage our sexual experience to be balanced with genuine affection.
____ I discuss openly with my spouse my religious beliefs.
____ I encourage my spouse to pray, worship, and pursue spiritual growth.
____ I encourage our marriage to be influenced by our spiritual goals.
____ I allow my decisions to be influenced by my mate.

_____ TOTAL

Low RQ		Average RQ		High RQ
60	120	180	240	300
Never	Seldom	Occasionally	Frequently	Very Frequently

1. Confront the cliché head-on. Consider the following dialogue from a book called *Nonverbal Communication and Marital Interaction* by Patricia Noller:

WIFE: "Bob, would you like something to drink or some ice cream?"

No answer.

"Bob?" she continues. Still, no answer.

Many wives would have abandoned any attempt at conversation at this point. I mean, think about it: speaking to a stone wall would be easier than this. But remember the first law of establishing intimacy: Breakthroughs Require Confrontation! If you want to remain where you are, do nothing. However, this wife in this example didn't require a written marriage manual to know how to reach to her husband. She merely spoke from her heart: "Look honey, I know you well enough to know that when something is wrong you often withdraw, you don't talk about it, I can't get anything out of you. I'm not the kind of person who can go on like that. I've got to explode and get it off my chest and talk about it. Now, something has been wrong for several days. Bob, is anything wrong at work? Have I done anything? We can't go on avoiding the situation. Please listen. Stop pouting, and tell me what's wrong."

BOB: "Did you feed the cat?"

WIFE: "Yes, but that has nothing to do with what we're talking about. Please talk to me. Tell me anything that's wrong. What is the matter with you?"

BOB: (sighs) "You know what's wrong."

[The wife] replies again at length, denying that she knows what's wrong, pointing out that they can't have a healthy marriage ignoring one another, claiming that she loves him very much.

To all this he replies, "Did you let the cat out?"

The scene continues with her lengthy appeals to him countered either by his insistence that she knows what's wrong or his cool extraneous clichés ("Do you want a Coke?", "Did you cash the check?"). The scene ends with no resolution. . . .

But an essential step has been taken. One mate has put the other on "cliché alert" by refusing to participate any longer in the dance. By confronting the problem head-on, you can take a major step toward breaking the cliché cycle and moving toward deeper, more substantial ground. It might not happen on the first try, as the above example painfully illustrates, but what's important is the effort. Without effort, you'll forever remain talking about nothing.

2. *Challenge the unspoken cliché.* Let's go back to our newlywed couple, walking on tiptoes, terrified to disrupt their perceived perfection of marriage with—here's that dreaded word again—confrontation. But running away from confrontation is an open invitation to trouble. Avoiding it takes you nowhere, except into the limbo of clichés, until one mate seizes the cliché and breaks some serious emotional ice.

It isn't easy to break through the wall separating the cliché cycle and the next, deeper level of intimacy—sharing facts— but here is a baby step taken from the book *Encounter with Family Relations* by Wes Seelinger. It concerns a husband who dared to seize the unspoken cliché of newlywed bliss, a confrontation that was painful at first but eventually had tremendous impact on the growth of the marriage.

> Our wedding day was on October 14, 1966. But our marriage began three weeks later. We were dressed up and on our way to the swankiest restaurant in town. We had saved all week for the big splurge.
>
> One problem—my bride was wearing the most horrible perfume ever manufactured. Smelled like a mixture of mustard gas, black pepper, and vaporized maple syrup. I still get queasy thinking about it.
>
> We had stopped at a railroad crossing. It was cold outside. The windows were up and the heater was on. My nose and lungs silently begged for mercy. But I didn't want to upset my bride with a comment about her perfume.
>
> I had decided the one perfect marriage in history would be ours. No conflicts . . . no harsh words . . . no hurt feelings . . . no tears . . . nothing negative. My wife had made a similar resolution. For three weeks we had

walked on eggshells, protecting each other from the slightest unpleasantness.

Dare I break the spell? Dare I be honest and open? She had soaked in that blasted stuff every day of our marriage. I knew I couldn't hold out forever. So I said, in my sweetest, softest voice, "Honey, that perfume smells like bug spray."

Blammo! The husband seized the unspoken cliché that had kept his relationship flash-frozen in phoniness for three weeks since the marriage ceremony! The confrontation wasn't easy; it never is. But look how one moment of honesty eventually took this couple to a deeper level of intimacy. Our husband remembers his wife's initial reaction:

Silence! Like the silence that must have followed President Roosevelt's announcement that the Japanese had bombed Pearl Harbor. I stared straight ahead trying to concentrate on the steady, metallic rhythm of the train cars rolling by.

I glanced at my bride out of the corner of my eye. Her lower lip was quivering slightly. The way it still does when she's fighting a good cry.

We drove on. After an eternity, she mumbled softly, "I won't use that brand again."

Any married person can finish this story. We choked down our gourmet dinner. Pouted. Went through the "it's all my fault, Honey" routine. Shed tears. And were finally reconciled, promising never to be cross with each other again.

The whole episode is now part of our family lore. Our repertory of delightful "young and dumb" stories.

But I still think that our marriage began with my observation about the perfume. At that point we began to grow. We discovered marriage is a union stronger than emotions. We began to drop the foolishness about unruffled bliss. We took our first steps toward learning that one all-important lesson, a lesson no one ever outgrows—love is a death-resurrection relationship.

As for the perfume . . . I sprayed the rest on roaches. It worked!

This story is proof that relationships are like those tiny glass snow globes enveloping miniature landscapes. Nothing happens until you shake them up! Forget the myth of "unruffled bliss." Optimum relationships require the courage of confrontation. If you notice an unspoken cliché—phoniness, pretension, artificiality—seize it, confront it, shake it up and you'll take your relationship to a deeper level.

3. *Turn a cliché into a fact:* You already know the general direction of the ultimate relationship roadmap. From the shallowest level (speaking in clichés), the goal is to move deeper to the next level (sharing facts). How do you make this integral move? Start by making a conscious decision to move from clichés to facts every chance you get.

Consider our original example of clichéd conversation. Remember the couple who were caught on the "How was your day?—Fine" merry-go-round? They will never achieve a deeper level of communication until one of the partners stops, recognizes the clichés for what they are, and transforms them into facts. That's not as hard as it sounds. Let me show you how it works.

"How was your day?" a wife asks her husband.

"Fine," replies the husband. Instead of reverting to the cliché of another question ("How was work?") that the husband will surely answer with an equally empty answer, the wife could instead turn the cliché of his previous answer ("Fine") into a fact by using drive-through listening, in which one partner repeats what he or she comprehends the other partner has said.

"So you're telling me your day was fine, without a single, solitary problem?" she could ask. "Well, that's wonderful, dear. Let's go out and celebrate."

The results of such an experiment in directed conversation can be astonishing. It's called a "pattern interrupt." In this situation, the husband most likely won't choose to hide behind another cliché. The wife has stated a fact and eliminated the possibility of a "fine" or "okay" answer. She's taken the tiny yet pivotal step from clichés to facts, and her husband has no choice but to rise to the challenge.

"Well, not exactly fine," the husband might reply. "There were actually plenty of problems." Now, the wife has moved her recalcitrant husband from sharing clichés to actually talking in facts! Don't drop the ball now! Take full advantage of the opening. Ask a meaningful question ("Tell me what the problems were"), in hopes that he will respond with a meaningful, factual answer. It may be only semantics, but words are the primary tools we have in the journey toward intimacy. Words not only precede action, they also dictate action. Use words wisely; they are your best friends in building a meaningful relationship and a successful marriage.

Words can actually enable you to "lead" your mate out of the level of clichés and into a deeper realm. If you're still stuck, here is one more technique to try.

Leading Questions

Just as the wrong words can keep your relationship mired in the mundane, discovering and utilizing the right words can deliver you from the darkness.

In the world of retail sales, several major corporations train employees to use a form of communication designed to get past clichéd communication between the sales employee and the potential customer. I believe this sales technique, called "leading questions," can offer couples importance guidance.

Just as mates frequently speak in predictable patterns, consider the normal Q&A played out in shopping malls across America.

SALESPERSON: *"Can I help you?"*
SHOPPER: *"No thank you. Just looking."*

In two quick sentences, the prospects for a sale—and a commission—are dashed. Savvy retailers train their employees to use a cliché-breaking skill that instantly creates more fruitful interaction with customers. Sales associates are discouraged from approaching store customers with dead-end questions such as "May I help you find something?" or "Can I help you find a size?"—basically clichéd questions that are easily answered with the clichés of "No" or "Just looking." Instead, sales associates are taught to ask "leading" questions that inspire a more thoughtful fact-oriented response. "What color are you looking for today?"

The customer certainly can't give a simple "No" answer to that!

Salespersons are instructed to "be specific" in their questions. "Are you looking for a loose fit or a more snug fit?" "What is the occasion you are buying for?" These types of questions actually lead a person to answer in complete sentences, often resulting in a more meaningful exchange.

It is the same in a marriage. Asking your partner leading questions will lead to more meaningful answers.

Be specific. Instead of asking a generalized clichéd question like, "How was your day?" try, "What's the price that the company stock was trading for today?" (He can't just answer, "Fine.") Or, "Who are you working with on the new deal?" (It's a question that requires specific names and explanations.) Or, "When do you think things will quiet down enough to take off for our two-week vacation?" (Requires more than just an easy answer.)

Your mission is to challenge your mate without being pushy, intrusive, or nagging. It's a delicate science, but one that every person interested in optimum relationships has to learn. Ask leading questions. They'll eventually lead you to the deeper levels of communication—and little, seemingly insignificant steps eventually lead to major advances.

CHAPTER THREE

The Barren Conversation

Facts

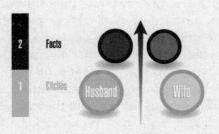

"Men do not exist in facts; they exist in dreams."
—Sherwood Anderson, "Memoirs"

ONE AFTERNOON I RECEIVED a 911 call, the relationship consultant's equivalent of a four-alarm fire. A local dentist had come home from work to discover his wife, who worked in his office as a dental hygienist, with her bags packed, her car gassed up, and her mind dead-set on leaving. She'd finally had enough of her husband's emotional distance, unresponsiveness, and inability to share his feelings. It was a scenario I've seen women suffering the world over. In their twenty-year marriage, this couple had not been able to escape the first two shallowest levels of intimacy: speaking in clichés and sharing facts. The marriage, like a plant without water, was literally dying of thirst.

On the surface, the husband was a pillar of the community, a nonstop blur of incessant motion, always the first to lead a civic or church committee, someone who would be your best buddy at the community cookout. But at home, stripped of his public persona, he was still the rejected son who was repeatedly told he was "irresponsible" and never received his father's approval, the boy who was kicked out of his childhood home at eighteen. He had devoted his life to proving his worth, which he eventually found through his work. Unfortunately, he had to pay a price. "If you ask your wife how you're doing in your relationship on a scale of 1 to 10, she'll usually rate you four or five points lower than you think you're doing," he says ruefully now. "Well, I was about 10 points lower, and I didn't even realize it. I got so engrossed in being successful, I neglected everything—including my wife."

The two had met in their mid-twenties when both were in dental school. Dating a year, they had a "storybook romance," then celebrated a storybook wedding and the storybook births of a boy and a girl. But along the way to the big white house with the picket fence and the two new cars in the garage, they forgot one crucial thing: each other. They went directly from their courtship and wedding into working together—and, before they knew it, their life together had gone from romance to routine. "We weren't communicating," she remembers. "We'd been going so fast, been used to going so fast, that we didn't realize that we hadn't been talking. We'd just been busy going. And being busy is a good coverup, if you just keep on going. Finally, I realized in my heart that when I was with him, he wasn't listening to what I had to say and wasn't interested in anything about me."

At home, in the car with their two young children, in restaurants, outside the church, and inside the mall, the dentist and his wife had an unspoken agreement: they'd speak only in facts, specific facts about the dentistry business they shared:

"I think that root canal went well today," he'd say.
"Well, you were able to get everything cleared up," she'd say.
"Yes, and the patient didn't seem to be in too much pain."

"She knew you were being as gentle as you could," she'd answer.

"I'm seeing the child with the three cavities tomorrow, right?" he'd ask.

"Yes. I'll put his records on your desk in the morning." she'd reply.

For thirteen years, they remained stuck speaking about dental facts—a never-ending routine of trading inarguable sentences about cavities, decay, crowns, and bridgework. Their life became a world of "what," "when," "where," and "how," but never "why;" "why" is too close to sharing an opinion, and opinions cause conflict—something they took great pains to avoid.

But deep inside this woman's heart, she felt the stirring, the deep, undeniable longing for *more*. Life, she felt, just had to be more than this never-ending robotic cycle of dentistry facts. So, she began trying, ever-so-subtly at first, to nudge her husband out of the fact habit and into deeper levels of conversation. "I kept pursuing and pursuing," she says.

"Initially, she'd try to bring up a conversation about the kids, or about her folks, or about us," he remembers. "But she finally recognized I didn't seem to have a clue about what she was talking about. So she would abdicate: *I know I can have some sort of conversation if I talk about work.* She so deeply wanted to talk to me about something, *anything*, she'd talk to me about work. But then she'd get frustrated. The time she wanted to spend discussing our relationship was spent discussing stuff: work, the projects, the next activity outside the house. Then, she finally realized she wasn't being true to herself."

They were caught in a web: the one-dimensional web of facts, which like the spider's web seems so unthreatening until you begin to get caught in it.

Sharing facts is the second level of intimacy, only one level deeper than sharing clichés. But it's just a baby step for a couple on the journey toward deeper intimacy. You and your mate are still offering each other nothing personal or intimate in your conversation. Yes, you're doing better than the

automatic-pilot babble of clichés, but you're really only trading information. If you're ever going to get to the deeper
levels—sharing feelings and needs—you'll first have to break
out of facts.

Here's how to begin.

Escaping the Prison of Facts

How do you break out of the superficiality of facts? You look
to the key aspect of the ultimate relationship roadmap: communication. As we've discussed, the language of love describes
the state of love.

In my interviews with women, I ask them, "Is there any
room for improvement?" If the answer is yes, the woman's pre-
scription for improvement is almost always the same: "If we
had better communication."

"What do you mean by that?" I'll ask.

And she'll tell me her definition of better communication:
moving beyond the stages of clichés and facts into the depths
of sharing feelings and needs.

But true communication doesn't come automatically. It
takes work. One reason is that our words serve myriad purposes: just as they can invite someone in, they can also keep
someone out. Nine times out of ten, if you ask your spouse the
simple question "How are you doing?" he or she will answer
with the most overused single-word fact in the English language: "Fine."

What a waste of time and potential emotion! Great relationships have the dialogue of the best cinematic love stories.
Think of your favorite movie romance. Most likely, it starred
two people who were in a constant volley of words. Bogie and
Bacall, Hepburn and Tracy, Meg Ryan and Billy Crystal, and,
most recently, Jack Nicholson's Oscar-winning performance
alongside Helen Hunt in *As Good As It Gets*. Would you have
sat in a movie theater for even two seconds to hear these cellu-
loid lovers speak in boring facts or clichés? Certainly not! You
paid to hear them rant and rage, battle over their opinions, repeatedly disagree, before they eventually agree on something

and, in the end, dramatically fall in love. The very thing that keeps them at odds—conflict—is the thing that eventually brings them together. That's what you pay to see on-screen. You watch them make the journey that you're going to make in this book, from surface dialogue to the depths where true love lives.

You pay to see love movies because, in many cases, you aren't experiencing it at home. Instead, you find yourself speaking in facts, the language of incontestable statements—statements about work, the evening news, the children's activities, the weather—uncolored by opinions, which, of course, inevitably lead to conflict. The fact-sharing couple stays entrapped in the "safety" of the statements they trade, rarely daring to delve, merely sailing on the surface of a real relationship.

In most cases, fact-sharing couples are not people without opinions—just people unwilling to share their opinions with each other. They might be afraid of each other's reactions. They might just despise conflict. But the problem is that unexpressed opinions and feelings do not go away, they simply find another outlet. And often the outlet through which pent-up emotions escape is not very pretty. Couples who "keep the peace" by holding their opinions to themselves often wake up one day and discover that they are absolute strangers.

Fact sharing is a form of substitution conversation, replacing anything real or honest with the mundane. At first, sharing facts might seem like an attractive way to keep a relationship going. Couples in this stage rarely fight or argue, and they often can carry on in this manner for years without incident. But I hope that you will soon see the fact-sharing level of intimacy for what it truly is: a safe corner of a boxing ring where couples hide before the bout of living even begins, a lifeless place of neither victory nor defeat, a place where your relationship can remain stranded for years and even decades. Decades become lifetimes, until the credits of your life's movie roll. The words "The End" flash on-screen and you turn to each other and say "Could it really be over so soon?"

The Three Descending Levels of Facts

I've discovered that there are three species of facts, which can become three stages of a slowly decaying relationship.

Facts as Words

The first stage of fact sharing is something all relationships go through; it's the tap dance before the ballet, the warmup before the big show. We get to know our mates through facts, and sometimes facts also lead us to love them. But we come to truly love them through sharing opinions, feelings, and needs. There are two types of verbal facts: household and nonhousehold. Household facts include statements about the daily functions of the home and family—what grade the son or daughter got on his or her spelling test; something funny the dog did that day; how much the repairs on the roof will cost. Nonhousehold facts include everything from facts about work to the world at large, but usually minus the minefield topics of politics and religion, subjects that usually bring forth opinions, which at least one partner in the fact-sharing couple is determined to avoid.

The couple sharing "facts as words" might have a dinner-table conversation like this:

> "Did you talk to the pool company today?"
> "They are coming out to fix the drain on Wednesday."
> "When are you going to the grocery store?"
> "Tomorrow."
> "We need milk when you go."

This husband and wife are definitely talking, but not about anything personal. Each partner expresses no opinion about what is being said. The two are simply trading information with each other. The responses given in return are neutral and predictable. This existence is perfectly pleasant—and perfectly empty. Although the absence of negative emotion is safe, the absence of any emotion at all is disturbing. If these two disagree on anything, no one would ever know by their conversations.

However, the emotions and feelings that go unsaid in factual conversations don't go away. The couple who do not find a way to break out of the "facts as words" stage often soon find themselves in the next, more dangerous stage—"facts as actions"—where a fact cannot be denied.

Facts as Actions

You've certainly read about relational "facts as actions" in the headlines, at least the headlines of the celebrity press. Consider the movie star who leaves his wife for another woman. *It is an action portraying a fact: what he or she was getting at home wasn't enough to keep them there.*

Think of the once-again-divorcing television personality who is once again checked into the Betty Ford Clinic. *The fact: either the alcohol is causing trouble in her marriage or the trouble in her marriage is causing the alcoholism.* Then there is the actress diagnosed with anorexia, a woman loved by everyone, except her mate. *The fact: her physical starvation is a direct manifestation of the emotional starvation in her marriage.*

Think of all the facts as actions that never hit the headlines: "Jane Doe cries her eyes out a dinner party." *The fact: husband's insensitive comments finally take their toll.* Or, "John Doe storms out of house." *The fact: uncommunicative wife finally put on notice.*

What you don't say to each other will eventually find a route of expression. When a fact—especially the fact that one mate is unfulfilled—finds its voice through action, then it's time to take control of the situation and communicate—really communicate. Without communication, the mate who desires deeper levels will begin stating facts as actions—and those actions will hurt.

Certainly, you have heard someone contemplating turning a fact into an action: "She won't talk to me. I'll find someone who will." "He wants to commune with the television set night after night? I'll communicate with a bottle of Tanqueray." "He won't open up. I'll open up another box of cookies or another tub of ice cream."

Facts as actions are painful, destructive, and ultimately embarrassing. Attempt to communicate with your mate before you get to this level. If you're acting out the facts of a uncommunicative relationship, realize it for what it is—a response to a deeper disappointment—and seek help, first from your mate, then if that's not possible, from a professional therapist.

Facts as Silence

When facts, especially facts of unhappiness or unfulfillment, are expressed in silence—when you cannot trade even the most banal information with your mate—then the relationship has reached a potentially critical point. The silent partner is most likely raging with his or her unhappiness internally. He or she can do this through inner talking, a concept that I will explain more thoroughly later in this chapter.

Consider a woman in this silent stage: "When I try to bring up the subject of my feelings and thoughts, I'm cut off," she says. "He'll interrupt me and try to go to another subject. He doesn't want to listen to me. When he does, it's only to put me down. In times past I would take his neglect and try to respond with something positive. But now I'm more inclined to say nothing. I'll think, 'He's impossible. Why have another fight with him? Just let it go.' "

Once your mate is conveying the fact that she is unhappy through silence, it's time to seek professional help. If you don't, that silence is eventually going to explode. And by then, it will be too late to do anything.

What's Hiding Behind the Facts?

If you're in a relationship with a compulsive fact sharer—or if both of you are stuck in the fact-sharing stage—remember this: facts always convey a deeper meaning, an unspoken message. Facts are merely the envelope in which your mate is carrying something else, something deeper. The dentist described at the beginning of this chapter was literally hiding his emotions behind a veil of cold, protective facts. Looking deeper, I discovered that he was hiding the lingering sting of never having received his father's acceptance, the pain of being kicked out of his parents' house at eighteen, and his insecurity about being a successful dentist, husband, and father. He hid all of his pain behind the factual conversation about dentistry—and only dentistry—that unconsciously and successfully kept both his wife and his pain at bay. He wasn't a bad man, just like a million others looking *outside* themselves and their homes for happiness, not realizing that what mattered was *inside*.

We all search for some source of significance, happiness, and purpose, which—at least in Y2K America—most people believe can best be found in people, places, and things: the right vacation, the right friends, the right possessions. But these things don't provide the contentment or purpose that we are really searching for. We yearn to be recognized as unique, to feel loved for all our strengths and weaknesses, to be *completely known* by someone else and, more importantly, *completely accepted*. Only when emotionally tied to someone else can you have a mutually satisfying marriage. But we are never taught that emotional intimacy is our most basic need. We are instructed to look for "things" to fill our time instead of feelings to engage our hearts. We cling desperately to false beliefs: that success brings happiness, that "things" bring joy, that wives and husbands are people, not oceans to dive into until we reach the bottom where the true treasure lies.

Of course, most people don't realize these truths until it's too late. They think that as long as the relationship is humming along, as long as there is a connection through sex, everything is fine. This is an especially prevalent attitude among men. It's been said that men will do anything for sex, even love, while women will do anything for love, even sex. In the case of our distracted dentist described at the beginning of this chapter, he just got so caught up in the "trappings" of proving his worth, of being successful, that he quite literally left his wife and family behind.

No matter how hard his wife pursued him, the dentist

kept running away. At home at night, he'd hide his mind inside the constantly blaring television, channel-surfing and half-heartedly listening to his wife as she rambled on as background noise. To her probes, questions, and comments he'd answer, "Okay," "That's fine," and "Sounds good," shallow yet agreeable decrees to cases he never took the time to hear.

Finally, his wife came up with a compromise, a pact. They'd agree not to talk about dentistry when they were out of the office. Trying to avoid conflict at all costs, he agreed to try. So she'd bring up personal family things. She'd encourage him by suggesting a night out, saying, "Let's cut loose and have a little fun." But he was determined to stick with facts. Even on their one night out to dinner together, he'd revert to facts: the inefficiency of the waiter; the quality of the steak; factual dissections of restaurant time management, and the importance of location and interior design. "I could not relax," he remembers today. "I was just so caught up in being successful."

Finally, his wife's frustration reached the breaking point. "You're not taking any time for us," she said. "Everything you're doing either involves work or some other volunteer effort—the church, the community. When is it going to be *our* time?"

He answered, of course, with facts, with his brain instead of his heart. "Honey, I'm supporting you," he replied. "I'm providing you with a good lifestyle. We came to town with nothing. I got booted out of the house when I was eighteen. Look at what I've done. Why aren't you more appreciative of the stuff I've given you?"

"I don't want stuff!" she screamed. "I want *you*!"

When she pursued him, when she dared to challenge him, he had a quick and easy way to cut her off: sarcasm. He wielded his language like a weapon. "I could stop a conversation through sarcasm, just by saying something cutting," he remembers. "I was sharp enough to say something that would make her stop. I was more willing to let her be angry with me than to get into an intimate discussion, where she could see how much I was really hurting."

Think about it. One critical remark from her husband and she'd retreat. "She'd get upset with me, then I'd get upset more and then we'd just stop talking until we started talking about work again," he remembers.

But the facts were merely a shield, behind which the dentist had hidden his overwhelming pain. "Share my feelings— why would I do that?" he says today. "That would have made me vulnerable. If I was insecure as a male, and I was covering up my insecurity by being a success in my business, why would I let my wife know that? No way! I had to keep up that front. If she saw that I was suffering and if she tried to pull that out of me, then my defense was to get angry. So I wouldn't have to go to that level of intimacy."

His heart was wound and bound, like a ball of string; he felt that one successful pull would dizzily unravel the whole spool and leave him emotionally exposed. So he hung onto facts for dear life—until, eventually, his wife presented him with a fact of her own. She was leaving him.

Beyond the Facade of Facts

How do you rescue your relationship from the never-ending cycle of sharing facts? Slowly and subtly. Consider this example of a wife gently forcing her husband to break out of the fact-sharing mode. It might be as simple and short as:

"Honey, where do you want to go out to eat tonight?" she asks, her very question demanding an opinion, instead of merely a fact.

"Well, the options are sushi, Mexican, Thai, or Italian," he replies, resorting to facts.

"I know what the options are, dear," she answers. "But where do *you* want to go?"

"Sushi is closest, and the Mexican place will be crowded," he says, still stuck in the fact mode. "We've never been to the Italian place. I'm not sure if the Thai place is open tonight."

"But where do you want to eat?" she repeats.

"Either sushi or Mexican," he replies, finally with a

decision. "But given the choice, I think I'd rather have Mexican."

A small victory, but a nonetheless essential one. She has forced an opinion out of him.

"Great!" she replies. "Mexican it is. I would prefer that, too."

Steering your mate from facts to actually sharing an opinion is a seemingly small yet vital step toward intimacy. Do not let this act go uncelebrated. Every time you catch him or her moving one step beyond the level where you are, and towards the territory of intimacy, speak up! *Catch the person doing something right.* Then praise the heck out of him or her for it. I'm talking about celebrating small things: the tiniest opinionated response, the most subtle move toward deeper communication. Because small steps add up!

Catch Your Mate Doing Something Right

You can actually guide your mate's actions with your attention, interest, and praise. Remember, it's not only women who have a need to be noticed, praised, and celebrated. Men seek affirmation just as vigorously, although they sometimes go about it in different ways.

Now, you may be thinking that it's impossible to "steer" or "sway" your stubborn mate. After all, if you can't get him off the couch, how are you going to lure him into the deepest end of the pool of intimacy? I've discovered that human beings can be steered simply through attention. And I have proof. It's as old as Psychology 101, where students in an example I recently read about proved that it is possible to influence someone's behavior. They had been discussing the power of nonverbal praise and decided to conduct a test, using their teacher as a guinea pig.

In the corner of this classroom stood a hot water radiator

that the teacher routinely got up from his desk to walk toward. The students decided that when the teacher began lecturing, at his desk, they'd act bored. But when he started walking toward the radiator, no matter how interesting the lecture, they would perk up. They would begin taking furious notes, flashing each other interested looks, nod their heads in enthusiastic agreement, even say words like "Whoa" to convey their interest and enthusiasm. Whenever the teacher moved away from the radiator, they would look bored, doodle on their paper, stare at their watches, check the clock, even fall asleep.

Within three weeks, the class had the professor *seated* on the radiator. They didn't really care what he was saying, but their reaction made him move toward the place where they seemed to notice him most.

Maybe you can learn something from these psychology students. Is it possible that a little positive feedback from you could incite a positive response from him or her? Maybe, all you need to do is show some interest to have the person return some interest and attention to you. Your attention has power! It can literally move people.

How do you best employ the power of attention? One effective way is through praise. Praise your mate for the small things, because small things eventually add up to big changes. I've discovered some husbands and wives who expect big, life-altering results before issuing even the slightest praise. They think, "If I don't get praise when I unload the dishwasher, why should I praise him for unloading the dishwasher?"

That mentality is part of the problem, not the solution. Words carry charges, both positive and negative. We'll discuss positive and negative charges at length in a later chapter, but I'd like you to begin thinking of their significance now. In my interviews with women around the world, most said they get charged when they have security, when they are told they are loved and treasured, when there is daily communication. They get positively charged when they feel understood and validated. They get charged if they're doing things with their mates, going places and participating in activities together as a couple. They get charged by their mates' touch. These are key charges—and they're important to remember, especially when you are trying to break out of the fact stage.

So put these words on a sign in your brain: *Catch your partner doing something good and praise the heck out of it!*

Your Inner Voice

Have you ever found yourself engaged in a conversation in your own mind? Everybody does. In many instances, it is a good way to work a problem out in your own head, to clarify arguments or sort out jumbled emotions. But when it comes to relationships, inner talking is an integral part of the ultimate relationship roadmap; it's a natural tool you can use to break you and your partner out of the fact habit and on to the more satisfying levels of sharing opinions, feelings, and, ultimately, needs. You are most likely already using this mental tool; we all mentally analyze conversations before speaking them aloud. But it took a woman whom I had the great fortune to be seated next to on an airplane to show me how this process can aid the journey to deeper intimacy.

"I do a lot of inner talking," she told me. And when she began telling me about inner talking, I knew she was describing yet one more aspect of the ultimate relationship roadmap.

"It's an automatic reaction," she continued. "I take what I've heard him say and transpose it from something bland or negative into something positive. If I didn't do inner talking, we'd have been divorced a long time ago."

She has been married more than thirty years, she said. Many times, she and her husband would get close to a breakthrough: sharing opinions, which invariably cause conflict, and then—*bam!*—they'd each retreat, like exhausted soldiers calling a temporary truce, to the safe terrain of speaking in clichés and sharing facts.

But while reverting to sharing seemingly mundane facts with her husband, this woman, whom I will call Patty, is having an inner dialogue with herself. She does it not only for control—to keep from blowing her top with her husband—but also for emotional sustenance. Because in a relationship, speaking in facts is like eating snow: it'll quench your thirst, but there's absolutely no nourishment in it. Speaking in facts is a not-so-artful dodge, a way of verbal fencing without touching swords. Beneath the deceptively calm waters of factual interchange, at least one mate is a raging river of inner conversation, wondering when, where, and how to get the recalcitrant partner to talk, really talk, about things that matter. I hear the complaints the world over, in infinite languages, but with singular sentiment: "We are on this earth a finite number of years," all these people seem to be saying. "To waste even a moment of the time we've been given with this person with whom we've decided to share our lives is a slap at the grace of God that put us here."

So many television marriages—
that playing out of lives against a
background of the tube.
Instead of two lives filling the room,
There are two lives and the eleven o'clock news
With
Constant commercial interruption.
Instead of what you say and what I say
It's what Dick and Johnny and their guests say.
You don't laugh with me;
I don't laugh with you.
All the wit comes pouring out of the tube.
And we laugh at it together.
The more we avoid talking
The more passive our relationship becomes.
Television permits us to walk through
Life
With minor speaking parts.
And the more we fail to speak,
The more difficult speaking becomes.
                    —Lois Wyse, Lovetalk

The Power of Inner Talking

When the fact-sharing stage of intimacy drags on too long, when couples cannot move to the deeper levels, then inner talking becomes a defense mechanism. If one of the partners refuses to engage in meaningful conversation, the other can turn to inner talking to fulfill those needs, and eventually, to tune his or her mate *out*. This type of inner talking is the calm before the typhoon. Once this degree of inner talking begins manifesting itself in your marriage, the mate who's doing it is eventually going to emotionally explode. The inner talk will eventually become outwardly expressed and as we'll see later, the person on the receiving end won't be able to hide behind a facade of facts anymore.

Let me show you how Patty and her husband allow inner talking to replace a real conversation between the two of them. Beneath Patty's sunny exterior is a woman in *want*, a woman who, for thirty years, would walk from the living room where the man she'd dedicated her life to sat cold as a stone staring into a robotic box and stumble into her bed where she'd cry herself to sleep. But every night, she'd return to the living room stage where their little drama would play out, where she'd try and try again.

"What do you want to do tonight?" she'd ask.

It's a fact in the form of a question, the subtext asking: "We have this night to spend together. How are we going to use it?"

Her unspoken conversation, her inner talk, would be even more specific: "I'd say to myself, 'Let's get out of this room and go, do, or be something other than what we've done for most of the nights of the last thirty years."

She recalls, "I'd be thinking, 'Turn that TV off, flush the remote control, grab my hand, and talk—truly talk—to me!' "

"I want to watch the game," he'd reply, stating another fact.

He's doing his own form of inner talking, of course, even though he might not realize it. His inner talking goes something like this: "I've had a hard day at the office. My favorite team is playing tonight and I'm going to sit here and watch this game."

"We could go for a ride," she'd suggest, while her inner talking is screaming, "Maybe, if I can get him out of here, we can share something more substantial than the game scores."

"But it's the playoffs!" he'd reply.

I'm not suggesting it's always the man who is in the avoidance mode. Many a woman is parked in front of the television, while her mate is doing the inner talking to try and break her out. What's important to realize is that conversation is not what it seems; it always conveys a deeper meaning, a deeper need.

Of course, Patty could wait until she is about to burst with frustration and anger, then blurt out her opinion, leaping directly from sharing facts to the next, deeper level of intimacy—sharing opinions—in one single bound. But this is not the most effective route to the deeper levels. Think about it. If she screamed, "I'm sick and tired of your night-after-night addiction to the television!" that takes them immediately from sharing facts to critical comments (hers), followed by his almost certain condescension ("Who are you to tell me what I'm doing wrong?"). Then, two things can happen: one partner will leave or they will both retreat to the seemingly safer levels, speaking in clichés and sharing facts, until they gradually escalate into full-blown conflict again. Not a wise move, but one that happens repeatedly in relationships.

The challenge is to use inner talking efficiently and positively. If Patty used inner talking to map out, literally, why she felt so frustrated with her husband's TV addiction and why she thought some time outside the house together would help them, then she could eventually have a calmer and more loving exchange with her husband. Instead of an angry proclamation, she could rationally suggest a compromise. Instead of blurting out her disgust for his television addiction, Patty could offer a fact of her own: "Honey, I know how important the game is tonight because it is the playoffs. I was hoping that at half-time, we could take a break and run out for ice cream. My treat." This way, Patty has shown her husband that she has already considered the game's importance, but that she would really like to make time for them to do something together, too. If he rebuffed her, she could counter by saying, "OK, well, then, tomorrow night I would like to make some time for us before the playoffs start—maybe we could go to the video store and pick out a movie to watch together this weekend."

Patty hasn't really moved out of the fact mode; she is merely using facts to the best advantage of the relationship. She has shown her thoughtfulness, she has controlled her anger, and she has opened up new avenues for conversation. Inner talking allowed her to do all of this by systematically considering all the possibilities ahead of time. Anticipating her husband's interest in the game—it is, after all, the sacred play-offs—also helps Patty show her husband that she can respect his wishes as well as hers. If Patty has any hope of coaxing her husband into understanding how much she needs his consideration, she must show him some as well. It's not the ideal situation, but it is a baby step forward toward the deeper levels of intimate communication.

Imagine the Ideal Until You Find it

Now it's time for you to start flexing your own inner voice power to create a more positive exchange between you and your mate. Here's how you begin.

1. *Imagine the most complete, meaningful, intimate conversation with your mate.* It doesn't matter that you haven't had it yet, just that you imagine what it could be, if it did happen. Dream it up while you are taking a walk, on the treadmill at the gym, or even waiting for that red light to change. The important thing is for you to identify what you are yearning to receive from your mate and then play it out in your mind, using inner talking.

2. Praise your mate every time he or she gets even close to the intimate conversation you imagined. Once you've imagined the type of intimate conversation you're yearning for, you can actually guide your mate toward deeper intimacy by using praise. Every time you feel that he or she has come anywhere close to bridging the chasm between you—anytime you can

think, "Wow, that was pretty good!"—then praise your mate as much as you can. Smile. Hug him or her. Take him or her out to dinner. Do something that says, "We're moving in the right direction!" But do your "inner" homework first. Begin with inner talking, because if you don't know what it is you're looking for, how can you ever find it?

Insert Yourself into the Facts at Hand

Here's an exercise to help you steer your spouse into sharing noncombative opinions and to eventually break your relationship out of the vicious fact cycle.

Consider this conversation as an example:

> "What are you watching on TV?"
> "The playoff game."
> "Who's winning?"
> "The Yankees."
> "What are you doing after the game?"
> "I'm going to bed. I have to work early in the morning."

This couple is not communicating in any real way. Now watch: by adding just one sentence to each question, this wife could get him going in the deeper direction.

> "What are you watching on TV? I'll watch with you."
> "The playoff game."
> "Which team are you rooting for?"
> "I like the Rangers, but the Yankees are winning."
> "Uh-oh. What inning is it? Is there any way the Rangers can come back?"
> "The bottom of the sixth. Yeah, they have a fighting chance."
> "Well, after the game we'll go get some ice cream before you go to bed, and you can tell me about your day at work."

He may repeat his desire to stay with the game. But at least you tried to get him to go deeper. Don't ever apologize for it.

One Cursed Little Word

Now that you know it is possible to use the facts stage of intimacy in a way that's beneficial to the relationship, I'd like to give you a handful of words that have enormous power. On the plane, Patty told me about one of her husband's habits that she despises the most. No, it is not the TV or the avoidance or even their frequent arguments. Her disgust is over one little word, a seemingly ordinary word used in stating facts, but a word that is, to her, more vicious than any curse, a word that hurts her more than any verbal degradation. It's her husband's constant use of the word *me*.

"At this stage of our life, I'm approaching fifty-four and he just turned fifty-eight," she says. "He doesn't focus on the children anymore, he doesn't focus on me, he focuses on himself. In a simple conversation, he'll say, 'Well, I went to the store and I bought *me* a box of of cereal.' I just look at him like, 'Excuse me, there are two of us living in this house. The kids may be gone, but it's you and me.' If it was me, I would say, 'I went to the store, and I bought *us* a box of cereal.' "

Patty's observation hits upon an often-overlooked point: sometimes, our relational problems are as obvious as the words we use when we talk to one another. The isolation Patty and her husband have created is even showing up in her husband's language pattern, even at the shallow level of sharing facts. Unconsciously, he is pushing her out with that one little word: *me*.

Patty's husband's focus on *me* reflects a deeper problem in the marriage: he has withdrawn from the team that they had formed when they married. As Dr. Scott Stanley remarks in his book *The Heart of Commitment*, "A focus on 'me' leads to a focus on what I want, what I can get, and what you're going to give to me." That attitude pits Patty's husband against her, as if only one of them can have their needs fulfilled. "A marriage of me versus you is half a marriage at best," Stanley observes. "[It is] really more of a battleground for two individuals of the opposite sex than a field on which love is played out." He goes on to write, "A focus on 'me' naturally leads to a focus on what I want, what I can get, and what you're going to give me. A marriage of me versus you is half a marriage at best. . . ." In a personal conversation, Dr. Stanley recently added: "The pervasive emphasis on 'me' in our society is one of the most destructive forces in marriage imaginable. 'Us' makes for a great marriage, not 'Meism.' " Patty not only reacted to her husband's omission of *we* and *us*, but what the *me* language was really saying: she instinctively felt him isolating himself and distancing her.

How to Draw a Picture of Your Heart

There is another, even more powerful way to use facts to begin to deepen your relationship. By turning your facts into word pictures. I devoted the majority of my book *The Language of Love* to this very powerful conversation technique. I call it "emotional word pictures," and it's an extraordinary tool in communication, packing enormous emotion into an easily understood package. Word pictures empower facts and make them come alive. Word pictures push facts toward the next level of intimacy—sharing opinions—without the baggage of conflict that opinions inherently carry. They have the ability to open your mate's heart and allow him or her to instantly understand and feel what you have been trying—for months, years, sometimes even decades—to convey.

What is an emotional word picture? As I wrote in *The Language of Love*, a concise definition would be something like this: "An emotional word picture is a communication tool that uses a story or object to activate simultaneously the emotions and intellect of a person." Other names for this technique might be "extended metaphors" or "figurative language." In word pictures, you can put important facts about your feelings into familiar frameworks and common analogies so that your mate can relate to them instantly.

For example, here's a word picture from a woman describing her happiness in her marriage: "My husband treats me like a roomful of priceless antiques. He walks in, picks me up, and holds me with great care and tenderness. I often feel like I am the most precious thing in our home. He saves the best hours and his best effort for me, not the television."

Often, the most powerful word pictures can describe pain or struggle because they often have the power to make a mate wake up and immediately see the pain in his or her partner's heart. Consider this word picture from an unfulfilled wife:

"When I was first married, I felt like a beautiful, hand-crafted, leather-bound, gold-trimmed book that had been presented to my husband as a gift from God. At first I was received with great enthusiasm and excitement—cherished, talked about, shared with others, and handled with care. As time has gone by, I've been put on the bookshelf to collect dust. Once in a while he remembers I'm here. But if he would only take me off the shelf and open me up! If only he'd see how much more I have to offer him!"

What power words can hold! Properly presented, they can paint an absolutely credible picture of a person's heart. Suddenly, the fact of a neglected wife cannot be denied. When we convey facts through word pictures, we can grab our mate's attention and, more importantly, his or her heart and mind. We force the person to participate. Best of all, word pictures are like sharing facts: they convey meaning without being critical or accusatory. Word pictures diffuse criticism into an objective picture and allow a mate to understand facts and feelings without feeling criticized or accused.

Let me show you how word pictures broke down the facade of thirteen years of fact sharing that had separated the dentist and his wife we discussed at the beginning of this chapter. They had reached the critical impasse: facts as actions and facts as silence. He conveyed his facts as actions; he literally busied himself with so much work and outside activities that he left no time for his wife. She conveyed her facts as silence, turning him off, finally thinking to herself, "I'll never reach you. I give up."

Then, one day, I got a 911 call, the code word between me and my friends in my hometown of Branson, Missouri. If any of them find themselves at a critical impasse in their relationships, they can sound a 911 by phone and I'll drop everything and rush right over.

"She's leaving me!" the dentist shouted over the phone, sounding the 911 alarm. "Please, Gary, get over here quick!"

When I walked into his house that evening, there was an eerie silence in the room. The situation was critical. The wife, who for thirteen years had been unable to break her husband out of the fact-sharing mode, was ready to take their two kids and walk out on her husband forever. She had finally had enough; she just felt she could never convey her feelings to her husband. Nothing, she told me, could resuscitate their long-suffering marriage.

The dentist was confused. He didn't think he'd done anything wrong! And while his wife knew how she felt, she did not know how to convey her feelings to her husband.

In the midst of this stalemate, I asked the wife to construct a word picture, a description of the state of their marriage that her husband couldn't help but understand. I wasn't asking her to break out of the fact-sharing mode, only to skew it a bit differently. They had an unspoken agreement to speak only in facts about the dentistry practice they shared; so that's the tact we took.

"If your marriage was your mouth, what condition would it be in right now?" I asked her.

She took a deep breath. "Well, I'd say I have a cavity," she began. "It started out small. But it just kind of kept getting brushed over, again and again, and through time, it started eating through the enamel, working its way down into the bone. Eventually, I just let it go, and it got infected. If you let an infection like that go for a long time, eventually, it gets to your heart."

"And what's the name of that disease?" I asked her.

"Ludwig's angina," she replied.

The workaholic, "Just-the-facts-ma'am" dentist gasped.

"How far away from your heart is your infection?" I asked her.

"About an inch away," she said very certainly.

The distant dentist wasn't distant anymore. He was obviously shaken by his wife's description of their near-death relationship. Her word picture couldn't be denied; his wife was suffering from an infection that would surely destroy their marriage unless he did something—quick!

"Is this an emergency situation?" I asked him.

"Oh yes, absolutely," he said. "It can kill you."

She stared at her husband. "I have been coming into your office with this infection and all you do is give me a toothbrush and say, 'Stop complaining.' "

"What would you do if your patient had this problem, Ludwig's angina?" I asked him.

"Perform an immediate emergency root canal."

Then, something amazing happened. He physically broke down. Tears flooded his eyes. He rushed over to his wife, put his arms around her, and said, "Now I understand, and I'm sorry."

His wife's word picture had shown him her heart, the direction toward deeper intimacy that their relationship had to take.

But it was yet another word picture that helped her show him *how* he had to change.

"What would it take to cure the infection that is spreading from your tooth to your heart?" I asked.

She looked over at her husband and spoke from her heart.

"The antibiotic would be for you to stop the rat race, to slow down and discover who we are in this house," she said. "We need a husband and a father to focus on us. That's all it would take to stop the infection."

The word picture put the sad state of their relationship in a form that her husband could immediately comprehend. He could no longer deny the fact that his marriage was in serious—perhaps fatal—condition!

Now, take a moment to speak in word pictures with your mate. Here are five easy steps to help you.

1. Sit down with your mate and tell him or her to try a simple exercise with you.

2. Frame a message you've been trying to convey to your mate in a word picture, using the examples presented in this chapter.

3. Ask your mate to respond to you in an equally descriptive word picture.

4. Continue the dialogue in word pictures until each of you precisely understands how the other is feeling.

5. Finally, promise to follow through on the messages, desires, and directions your mate is conveying to you through word pictures.

The dentist had to pay special attention to number 5. The promise is always easier than the follow-through. His promise to change was just that: a promise, not yet translated into actions. "I couldn't really believe what I was hearing," the wife remembers. "It was what I wanted, but yet here was a part of me that said, 'Don't completely trust.' "

The husband was determined to show that he had the capacity to change, to grow deeper with his wife, but that wasn't easy. "The first time I started really listening to her, she asked me, 'Are you okay?' And I said, 'Yeah, I'm fine, why?' She said, 'Well, I don't know it just seems really strange that you're actually listening.' That was the first time that I just really sat and listened to her. She asked me if I was okay! I said, 'Yeah, I'm fine. I feel like I'm really listening to you.' "

"It was what I wanted for so long," remembers the wife. "But there was still a part of me, an inner voice that still said, 'Don't completely trust. Not yet.' "

It was a beginning. They had broken through the facade of facts and had delved one critical level deeper in the journey toward intimacy. But there was plenty of hard work ahead of them. Because when they left the shadow world of facts, they stood facing an even more imposing door, a virtual monolith that, in opening, would either fuse their hearts together forever or angrily rip apart what they had worked so hard to achieve.

They stood before the door to the third level of intimacy: the virtual passage to the deepest levels of love, the door of conflict.

I hope you find inspiration in their story. The dentist and his wife had experienced considerable emotional distance in their marriage. They had not been able to connect in a very long time. But it took only a moment of baring their souls to one another, being completely honest with both themselves and each other, to break down the wall of facts between them and get to the literal heart of the matter.

I want to share with you another testimonial, written by author Sue Monk Kidd. She experienced her own break-through, her own moment of light that came when she broke through the intangible barrier, reached out for her husband, and took his hand. Kidd and her husband stepped through the wall of conflict, and so can you. Here's her extraordinary story, one which I hope will show you what lies ahead for you, if you can only see conflict as a temporary barrier instead of wall:

On a mild summer day beside the sea, my husband and I were lying on our beach towels, reading, each locked in our own separate worlds. It had been like that a lot lately. We'd been busy, preoccupied, going in different directions. I'd hoped the leisure of vacation would be different, but so far we'd spent most of it marooned in silence.

I looked up from my book at the ceaseless roll of the waves, feeling restless. I ran my fingers through the sand. "Want to make a sand castle?" I asked my husband.

He didn't really, but he humored me. Once we got started, though, he became surprisingly absorbed in the project. We both did. In fact, after a while we were working over that heap of beach sand as if it was about to be photographed for *Sand Castle Digest*. Sandy made bridges across the moat, while I crowned the top of the castle with spires. We made balconies and arched windows lined with tiny angel-wing shells. It looked like Camelot.

Neither of us noticed when the tide changed. We never saw the waves slipping up until the first swish of water gnawed a little piece of our castle away. Indignant, we shored it up with sand and patted it down. But as the waves returned with monotonous regularity, our hands grew still and our eyes drifted off toward the horizon.

Sandy got on his beach towel. I got on mine. We went back to our silence.

The next time I looked around, the sand castle we'd labored over was awash in the shifting tide. The bridges were washing away and the spires were starting to lean.

I gave it a soulful look, an inexplicable sadness coming over me. And suddenly, in the midst of that ordinary summer, I had a moment of pure, unbidden revelation. There sits my marriage, I thought.

I looked at my husband. The soundlessness between us seemed to reach clear into the sky. It was the hollow silence of a mid-life marriage, a marriage in which the ceaseless noise of everyday living threatens to drown out the music of intimacy.

Dear God, when had the tide shifted? When had mortgages and laundry and orthodontist appointments become more important than those unspeakably long looks that we used to exchange? How long since we'd shared our hidden pain or stumbled together upon a joy that was round with wonder and laughter? How had it happened that two people who loved each other could allow such a distance to creep in?

I thought of the attentiveness we'd lavished upon our relationship in the beginning, and how, eventually, the demands and routines of running a household, raising two children, and juggling two careers had stilled our hands and averted our eyes.

That night, after the children were asleep, my husband found me standing in the shadows on the porch, staring at the night. "You've hardly said two words all evening," [he said].

"Sorry," I muttered. "I've just got something on my mind."

"You want to tell me what it is?" he asked.

I turned around and looked at him. I took a deep breath. "I'm thinking of us," I said. "I'm thinking that our relationship is being drowned out by the demands of day-to-day living. We've taken our marriage for granted."

"What are you talking about? We have a very committed marriage." He was indignant.

"Of course we have a committed marriage," I told him. "But sometimes it seems commitment is all we've got. Sometimes we are two strangers existing under one roof, each going separate ways."

He didn't say a word. Now I've done it, I thought. I've rocked the boat to the point of tipping over. I've told my husband our marriage is bordering on empty commitment. Good grief! We stared at each other. It was as if we were stuck inside some big, dark bubble of pain that wouldn't pop. Tears welled up in my eyes and started down my face. To my surprise, tears slid down his face, too.

And suddenly, in what is surely the most endearing moment of my marriage, Sandy took his finger and traced the path of my tears on my cheeks, then touched his own wet face, blending our tears together.

Strange how such things can begin to re-create the mystery of relatedness between two people. Sandy and I walked down the porch steps onto the beach under the blazing stars. Slowly we started to talk. We talked a long time. About the small agonies of being married, about the struggle of it all. We talked about the gnawed and fraying places in our marriage and how they'd happened. We spoke aching words about the unmet needs between us.

We were whirling in the darkness that had settled in our relationship. And yes, it was uncomfortable and scary, like bobbing around in the ocean without a boat. But trading chaos and braving pain is often the only way to come upon a new shoreline.

I hope this story will serve as an inspiration to you. Sue Monk Kidd and her husband were facing many of the same hurdles we have been discussing, and will be discussing in the remainder of this book—emotional distance created by an inability or a fear to talk about feelings; unmet needs; and communication problems. Only when they faced and overcame those hurdles together did they break through the wall into the deeper level of intimacy that awaited them. Just as Kidd realized that night at the beach, you will discover that you are not alone. Dare to reach out to your mate and tell him or her how you feel. You might be surprised by the reaction.

Now let's begin your dive into deeper, more satisfying levels. It lies just beyond the wall of conflict, and you can see it from here.

CHAPTER FOUR

The Wall of Conflict

The Wall of Conflict

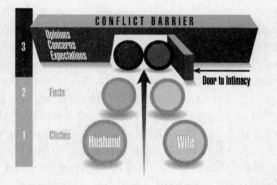

"I can't believe I married someone who has a different opinion than mine about almost everything."

—*Anonymous*

The Wailing Wall

"When will you be home tonight?" asks a wife.

"I don't know. I have to work late," replies the husband. "I don't think I can get home for dinner."

"Again?" says the wife. "You work too much."

Her opinion triggers an equally opinionated response from her spouse and, pretty soon, the opinions begin moving toward the wall like a slowly escalating freight train, all steam and smoke and charging steel.

"I have to work," he snaps. "I have to earn money."

"You don't have to," she snaps back. "You just do. You should tell your boss that you need fewer hours. You'll work yourself to death."

"I want to get ahead in the business," he says. "This is what I have to do to get ahead. I want to be a partner before I retire!"

"Is that all you care about? Your career? What about your family? Don't you care about us?"

"Why can't you support me? This is what makes me happy! I am trying to build a career! I am trying to get us all the things we want! How can you accuse me of not caring about the family? That is all I think about!"

The wall of conflict feels hot to the touch, fiery hot. You will find yourself staring up at it, its borders dark, infinite, and surrounded by barbed wire and "No Trespassing" signs. Shaking with fear and confusion, you'll react with the natural human fight-or-flight response to confrontation, the primitive, in-born reflex that urges us to either flee perceived danger or act against it in an extraordinary manner. First you will most probably attempt to fight it with brute force, but charging the wall is the *worst* strategy! Instead of moving forward, you'll be knocked backwards and off your feet. Your face will flush, your heart will hammer . . . your mind will be overwhelmed. You'll flee this reactional, emotional place and return to cooler ground. Only then will you be able to see the lunacy of what you've said and done, to—*of all people!*—the most important person in your life, your mate.

What's happening? You've stepped from the temporarily safe terrain of clichés and facts onto the third level of intimacy: sharing opinions, concerns, or expectations. These three land mines litter the third level of intimacy, their TNT detonated by conflict. Before you realize it, you'll be slamming your head against the wall of conflict, that place of knock-down and drag-out, where a simple disagreement can build up steam until it causes an explosion that can leave you and your partner burned and scarred.

Conflict is inevitable in relationships. It rears its head in even the healthiest, most deeply intimate of marriages. It is how you handle conflict that will determine how it affects your relationship, for better or for worse. Again, the most important aspect is not how much you love each other or how committed you are to your relationship or the strength of your faith; *optimum relationships depend on how adeptly you handle conflict.* Every instance of conflict represents two divergent paths: you can use it to either grow together or grow apart.

So you've come to a crucial point in your journey, a turning point. It is at this level of intimacy—learning to handle conflict, disagreements, arguments, or whatever you define as the act of having different opinions, concerns, or expectations from your mate—where you face the greatest danger. It is at this point that you can return to the superficial, less satisfying levels of intimacy or break through the wall of conflict and into the brave new world of intimate communication.

If you're going to dive to the deepest levels, *conflict is not only the wall, it's also the door.* Yes, conflict, handled constructively, is the power that can propel your relationship through the doorway that separates superficial relationships from profound ones. When you learn how to make conflict work for you, the doorway to intimacy swings open wide for you and your mate. It takes work, but every optimum relationship is the result of triumph over conflict.

The problem is, most couples don't see conflict as the doorway to a better, more satisfying relationship. In the full, red-faced flush of an argument, every bit of attention and logic is concentrated on "I'm-right-you're-wrong." They see the wall of conflict as a place of either victory or defeat, not a means for learning life's most valuable lessons. And so they fall before the wall, caught up in the force that is the universal destroyer of relationships: mishandled conflict. Then, they either find themselves in terminally shallow, superficial or mediocre relationships without any real joy or satisfaction or, even worse, experience the death of their relationships.

In this chapter, we're going to expose the true nature of conflict. We're going to drag it out of its hiding place, where, unexpected and misunderstood, it can leap into your life and wreak havoc with your relationship. But once understood and anticipated, conflict not only loses its power for destruction but also becomes a tunnel, a passageway to the two deepest levels of intimacy on the ultimate relationship roadmap.

> *"One of the myths is the idea that conflict is negative. . . . Nature doesn't see conflict as a negative. Nature uses conflict as a primary motivator for change. Imagine floating down the Colorado River through the Grand Canyon. Quiet water flowing into exhilarating rapids. Hidden canyons with shade trees and wildflowers. Clear springs of drinkable water. Solitude and silence that can be found in few places in today's world. And those majestic cliffs looming above, with fantastic patterns in the rock and all the colors of the rainbow displayed. The Grand Canyon is truly one of the world's greatest wonders and provides us with a profound sense of harmony and peace. Yet how was that amazing vista formed? Eons and eons of water flowing, continually wearing away the rock, carrying it to sea. A conflict that continues to this day. Conflict isn't negative, it just is."*

> —*Thomas F. Crum,* The Magic of Conflict

The Decision: Turning Your Swords into Plowshares

It is time to make a decision, one of the most important decisions of your relationship: how you view conflict. To make this decision, you and your mate are going to have to bravely step into the battlefield, onto the front lines that have mowed down many a couple. In the prophet Isaiah's words, you must "beat [your] swords into plowshares, and [your] spears into pruninghooks."

Most people view conflict as negative. Many can't stand disagreement in any form. And so, to avoid conflict, they avoid expressing their opinions and hope that their mate will do the same. But this mentality ends up stifling people—it makes them repress their true feelings and ignore their own uniqueness and individuality. Eventually, people resent each other for forcing such sacrifices of individuality. They suffocate what makes each of them special.

People who view conflict negatively react to it with fear, avoidance, anger, or frustration; when conflict arises, they attack the messenger instead of viewing conflict as a huge opportunity for change and progress. At the other end of the spectrum, mates who go straight for the jugular and react to conflict with anger often do as much damage to their relationships as do those who avoid conflict. Their hurtful attitudes go right at their mates with no attempt at tenderness or understanding.

Conflict: The Price We Pay for Intimacy

Dr. Gary Oliver once wrote about conflict: "No one wins in a world where we don't speak the truth in love, where conflict is denied or avoided or both. No one grows where the truth is absent, where no one is pushed to do and be the best. Without conflict, we remain relationally shallow. Intimacy can never develop. . . . Conflict is the price we pay for intimacy."

I love that line: "Conflict is the price we pay for intimacy." Without paying the price, the toll, we don't get to make the wondrous journey into the human heart. So make a conscious decision to embrace conflict as a natural and conquerable aspect of your relationship. Once you do that, your relationship will immediately begin moving toward deeper levels. Like the heads of long-battling nations, like forever-feuding mountain clans, only when you come to the table for dialogue can any real peace begin.

The Fork in the Road

You've reached a major turning point in your journey toward intimacy. It is at the third level of intimacy—the level of opening and sharing your heart—where the real work begins. At this level, you face the biggest decision of your relationship: how you will handle the conflict that naturally arises from expressing opinions, concerns, or expectations. If you can face conflict in a healthy, honoring way—which we'll discuss in later chapters—then you'll gain entry into the two deepest and most satisfying levels of intimacy. However, if you choose to react to conflict the way you always have, or the way most people do, then you'll most likely find yourself falling into the patterns of communication that weaken relationships and frequently lead to separation and divorce. The choice is yours.

If you have any doubt as to which direction to take, let me show you where the second road—the road of inaction or delay—can take you, a battleground well mapped by relationship experts Dr. John Gottman, Drs. Markman, Stanley, and Blumberg, and David Olsen.

> *"You cannot love or hate something about another person unless it reflects something you love or hate about yourself."*
>
> —*Cherie Carter-Scott*

Where Unresolved Conflict Will Lead You: The Four Main Risk Patterns for Divorce

Here's the important warning once again, from another source: "Contrary to popular belief, it's not how much you love each other that can best predict the future of your relationship, but how conflicts and disagreements are handled," wrote Howard Markman, Scott Stanley, and Susan L. Blumberg in their book *Fighting for Your Marriage.* I urge you to read this amazing book. In my view, this team is among the top five marriage experts and researchers in the world.

Markman, Stanley, and Blumberg discovered four distinct behavioral patterns that couples display in arguments that often lead to divorce. In fact, these behaviors are so prevalent in seriously troubled marriages that, if not resolved, they can lead to divorce. See if any of them is a frequent characteristic of your arguments:

- Withdrawal and avoidance
- Escalation
- Invalidating each other
- Having exaggerated or false beliefs about a mate

Let's examine them one at a time.

Withdrawal and Avoidance

"Withdrawal and avoidance are different manifestations of a pattern in which one partner shows an unwillingness to get into or stay with important discussions," say Markman, Stanley, and Blumberg. "Withdrawal can be as obvious as getting up and leaving the room or as subtle as 'turning off' or 'shutting down' during an argument. The withdrawer may tend to get quiet during an argument or may quickly agree to some suggestion just to end the conversation, with no real intention of following through. . . . Many couples do a kind of dance when it comes to dealing with difficult issues. One partner pursues dealing with issues and the other avoids or withdraws from dealing with issues."

They have identified two types of partners in conflicts involving withdrawal and avoidance: the pursuer, "the one in the relationship who most often brings issues up for discussion or calls attention to the need to make a decision about something"; and the withdrawer, "who tends to avoid the discussions or pull away during them."

"Studies show that men tend to take the withdrawing role more frequently with women tending to pursue," say Markman, Stanley, and Blumberg. "However, in many relationships the pattern is reversed."

It's easy recognize the pursuer and the avoider in an argument.

"I want to talk about our financial situation," says the pursuer. "I'm worried about making the house payments."

"I just got home from work," replies the avoider. "Can't we do this some other time?"

"I need to know what's going on. I want to be able to estimate our budget for the holidays."

"I'm just too tired to talk about this. Let's do it tomorrow."

"But, honey . . ."

"No! I don't want to talk! Can you ever quit bothering me? You are always bugging me!"

Let's consider a couple who recently began to heal the conflict that had almost torn their marriage—and their family—apart. Chuck and Liz have been married for almost twenty years, but most of them had been rough, according to Liz, because of issues left over from their childhoods. "We both had a lot of anger," she acknowledges now. "Growing up, we weren't taught to communicate."

As a result, Chuck and Liz had a hard time facing conflict in their relationship. "We both get very defensive and we close up quickly," notes Liz. With both of their defense shields erected, Chuck and Liz never really tried to resolve conflicts they encountered. "We would get hurt and insulted by each other, and we would just turn around and walk away," says Liz.

Liz says that since neither of them knew how to deal with conflict, they became afraid of it, screaming at each other instead of trying to communicate. Nothing would get resolved. The real problems were never faced. She wanted to try and heal their marriage, but she didn't know how to jump the barriers the two had set up between them. So their life became a stalemate; both parties afraid to speak to one another.

The habitual avoidance of their "real problems" eventually led Chuck and Liz to separate and prepare to get divorced. It was only when they faced conflict head-on that they could know each other fully—and to avoid the final effect of avoidance, which, for them and infinite other couples, was divorce.

The lesson? Avoiding conflict is not the answer! Yes, on a short-term basis it certainly feels less painful to avoid arguments, explanations, and analyses of your feelings and needs with your mate. But when you decide to spend your life with someone else, you must face the reality that you are not alone in the relationship. You and your mate's lives are intertwined. Your actions and emotions affect each other. If you seldom face conflict, or try to avoid even attempting to pass through the wall to the deeper levels, your relationship will remain stuck in the shallower levels of clichés and facts. You will never get the chance to know your partner completely, and more, you will never get the chance to be known yourself. You might stay married, but you might be forever alone.

Chuck and Liz finally reconciled, but only after they learned to see and handle conflict through a different perspective. Through the help of their pastor, they began dealing with conflict head-on. "We talk more now, we listen more, and we are more loving," says Liz.

They have learned how to ask for forgiveness and resolve disputes instead of just "walking away in anger," as they had in the past. "It's much easier now," she says. "We are so much calmer. We learned how to resolve the anger and the bitterness that got in the way for so long."

Adds Chuck, "Before, we made our jobs and our kids our top priorities. Now we know that the two of us have to be our first priorities on this earth."

Chuck and Liz made a decision, a decision you, too, will have to make to get to the deepest levels: to deal with conflict rationally. This decision will immediately allow the steam to escape from your relationship and for you to see your way clearly.

If you're stuck in this pattern of conflict avoidance, realize it's going to get worse unless you identify it and act immediately. Markman, Stanley, and Blumberg say, "That's because as pursuers push more, withdrawers withdraw more, and as withdrawers pull back, pursuers push harder."

To break the habit, realize that your withdrawal from an argument doesn't resolve it, instead it magnifies its capacity for destruction. If you're a withdrawer, learn to face the issues head-on. If you're a pursuer, then begin to pursue your mate constructively. Put a time limit on the amount of time the withdrawer can withdraw, but do give him or her some time to feel comfortable and less cornered. Act with kindness and tolerance and avoid blaming accusations and anger. In Chapter 6, we'll delve deeply into the idea of giving the withdrawer time to feel comfortable and less cornered.

Escalation

The second major pattern that certainly weakens marriages and can be a cause for divorce is escalation. "Escalation occurs when partners negatively respond back and forth to each other, continually upping the ante so that conditions get worse and worse," noted Markman, Stanley, and Blumberg. "Often, negative comments spiral into increasing anger and frustration."

Arguments that escalate out of control are the most dangerous type. Fear, pain, confusion—all of these forces build up steam and are expressed through negative, abusive words. Anyone who has ever been in a hellish argument knows that words can wound like weapons, and it is very hard to heal the scars they create.

As one happily married wife relates in *For Keeps*, a study of marriage and communication by Finnegan Alford-Cooper, "Once tempers go . . . the whole thing is finished . . . name calling or throwing things up to people. Those words, you can never take back."

"Partners can say the nastiest things during escalating arguments, but such remarks often don't reflect what they actually feel about the other," observed Markman, Stanley, and Blumberg. "You may believe that people reveal their true feelings in the midst of fierce fights, but we don't think that this is usually the case. Instead, they mostly try to hurt the other person and to defend themselves."

The authors noted that often, in the attempt to hurt each other, people will use against their mates information shared in earlier, intimate confidences. "Hence, the weapons chosen are often based on intimate knowledge of the partner," they note. "Such tactics are tantamount to marital terrorism and cause great pain and damage in the relationship. Who's going to share deep feelings if the information may be used later when conflict is out of control in the relationship?" they write.

It happens all the time: one ostensibly innocent remark sparks an escalating war of words:

> "Honey, please don't let the dishes pile up in the sink. Rinse them off and put them in the dishwasher when you're done."
>
> "I don't let them pile up, you do. I'm tired when I get home. Do I have to do everything around here?"
>
> "Do everything? You barely do anything! I have to do everything! Can't you help me at all?"
>
> "You could help me by making some money yourself so I wouldn't have to work so hard!"

Notice that the key word that does the most damage is the use of *you* in an accusatory manner. *You* can heat up any conversation; like a fuse, it ignites hurtful statements.

Here are some proven ways to halt escalation. First, identify escalation as a destructive force. Second, when you notice that an argument is escalating, be the one to stop, back down, and say, "Honey, let's take a look at what we're doing to ourselves!" My wife and I have agreed to set a boundary whenever we find ourselves getting out of control in a conversation. One of us will say, "This is not acceptable to me." Or, "I don't like the direction this conversation is headed. I'd like to take a break from it now." It's important to establish an agreement between you and your spouse to take a "time out." Otherwise, the "pursuer," the mate who is most avidly attempting to sell his or her point of view, can get really upset and attempt to continue the conversation through further aggression. We've also found that if we soften our voices and acknowledge each other's opinions, concerns, and expectations, we both tend to feel better, even when the conflict has not been resolved.

As one husband observes in *For Keeps*, "It requires constant vigilance. All too easily arguments can escalate. They feed upon themselves. One or both of us just quiets down . . . most of the time, we have the biggest arguments about the most trivial things."

In our case, Norma and I have both realized that we wrecked too many potentially fun times by arguing about something that didn't have great significance. We came to this realization by becoming aware that we never seemed to revisit the "earth-shattering subjects" that we delayed arguing about until we came home from our vacation. Learn to erect a similar shield against escalation in your relationship. It will take you one step further along the ultimate relationship roadmap.

Invalidation

The third risk pattern to avoid is invalidation. "Invalidation is a pattern in which one partner subtly or directly puts down the thoughts, feelings, or character of the other," write Markman, Stanley, and Blumberg. "Sometimes such comments, intentionally or unintentionally, lower the self-esteem of the targeted person. The argument settles into an attack on character sometimes. Another subtle form of invalidation occurs when you are expecting praise for some positive action that is ignored by your partner, while some minor problem is highlighted. Invalidation hurts. It leads naturally to covering up who you are and what you think, because it becomes just too risky to do otherwise. People naturally cover up their innermost feelings when they believe they will be 'put down.' "

This is the devil lurking in the closet, the fear that so many mates have that their deepest feelings, values, and desires will be ridiculed by their mates. Relationship expert Dr. John Gottman says belittling your mate is the number 1 cause of divorce, the absolute biggie. He calls this type of conflict "contempt." It's the polar opposite of honor, or placing high value on your mate. And it can begin whenever you feel that you're in some way better than or superior to the man or woman with whom you've decided to spend your life.

"Did you see that new Brad Pitt movie? It was so good! I loved it!"

"Are you kidding me? It was terrible! They shouldn't be allowed to make such stupid movies."

"What do you mean? I thought it was so moving. I am still thinking about its message."

"Message? The only message that movie sent was in Brad Pitt's biceps. I can't believe you're so simple-minded that you would be taken in by that stupid plot."

"It wasn't stupid! It was a love story!"

"Whatever. I can't talk to you. You're just like the rest of the dumb public."

To end invalidation in your relationship, practice its opposite: validation. Validate your mate through respect. This, to me, is the greatest skill, the skill that we will cover in the next chapter: the skill of honoring. This happens when you listen to your partner's concerns, values, and beliefs and validate them. "You don't have to agree with your partner to validate his or her feelings," say Markman, Stanley, and Blumberg. "Validation is a powerful tool that you can use both to build intimacy and to reduce anger and resentment."

In *For Keeps*, one wife explains how she and her husband avoid invalidation: "If I have something causing me a problem," she says, "when I present it to him he listens very patiently. He doesn't say, 'OK, now I'm going to do something different,' but I can see that he does do something different. Which says to me that he values what I say. We've learned from each other when we have disagreements, the techniques that we each use, so if he presents me with a response so that we have a kind of level playing field, it's not all hyperemotional. It's pragmatic, it's practical, it's good communication."

My wife and I discovered how very subtle this pattern can be. We found ourselves saying little things like, "Come on, give me a break, that's pathetic"—seemingly small comments that we never noticed until we started seeing how destructive they are. We stood back and actually listened to how we were talking to each other. We heard ourselves uttering these belittling statements that could have led us further down that dark road to a weakened relationship without us even knowing how we had gotten there! Without marriage researchers like Drs. Markman, Stanley, and Blumberg, the average spouse—like me—would never recognize when he or she is slipping into the danger zone.

Negative Interpretations

The last destructive pattern in marriage is definitely not the least. It is an emotional fungus that can grow on your relationship, *because what we believe in our mind always affects how we see and hear something.* Negative interpretations occur when one partner consistently believes that the motives of the other are more negative than is really the case. Think about this for a moment: your marriage may be suffering from a negative interpretation about you that your spouse is still silently harboring after months, years, even decades of being together!

I tell my seminar participants that one negative interpretation many wives hold is that their husbands lay in bed at night dreaming up ways to weaken their marriages. This is not true of most men! In my experience, men do not premeditate the destructive behavior they sometimes display in relationships. They are simply not as in touch with their "relational sides" as women are. Of course, I cannot speak for all men, but in my personal experiences, men have often overlooked the smaller, intimate actions that can help make a marriage a loving environment, but this certainly does not mean that they are aware of their oversights. Wives must try to keep an open mind and realize that the average man does not have the same "natural ability" to see and know the subtleties of intimate relationships that most women seem to have been instinctively blessed with!

"When relationships become more distressed, the negative interpretations create an environment of hopelessness and demoralization," write Markman, Stanley, and Blumberg. "Negative interpretations are very destructive, in part because they are very hard to detect and counteract after they become cemented into the fabric of a relationship. This intractability has its roots in the way we form and maintain beliefs about others. . . . In distressed relationships, partners have a tendency to discount the positive things they see, attributing them to causes such as chance rather than to any positive characteristics of the partner. The bottom line with negative interpretations is that positive behavior is viewed negatively, and negative behavior is seen as an extension of character flaws, even if the actual intention was positive."

Negative interpretations are subtle, but you can hear them creeping into arguments, like an incessant backbeat. Listen to the woman's negative interpretation—that her husband is ashamed of her—in this argument that seems to be about a Christmas party.

"When is your company Christmas party?" she asks. "I want to mark the calendar."

"Uh . . . I don't know," he replies. "I don't plan on going."

"What do you mean? It's your company's only social event of the year! Don't you want to go? I want to meet the people you work with!"

"I just don't get the point. The party is never any good, people act silly . . . I'd rather just stay home."

"Are you ashamed of me? You don't want me to meet them, do you? Why not? What's wrong with me?"

"That's not it. I just don't feel like going. We could go away for the weekend or do something fun instead. I see those people every day and I just dread those things."

"That can't be it. You're ashamed of me and you just don't want to tell me. You think I'm not smart or pretty enough."

"I don't know what you are talking about!"

The negative interpretation is unspoken by the man, but perceived by the wife and magnified. Be on constant guard for ways your mate could construe your comments negatively. Are you hypercritical of your partner? If so, stop it before it becomes a pattern. Keep an eagle eye out for evidence that disproves your negative interpretation, not enhances it. For instance, if the woman's husband in the conversation above ever praised her appearance or asked her opinion on an issue, she would be able to use those moments to wipe out negative thoughts in the aforementioned conversation.

Do you employ any of these four main divorce patterns when you fight with your mate? Are you a withdrawer, a pursuer,

someone with negative interpretations or destructive precon-
ceived ideas? If so, recognize it, discuss it with your mate, and
make a conscious decision to rid your relationship of these
dangerous practices.

Completing Each Other

The key to understanding why the four main risk patterns for
divorce are so damaging is that each creates anger inside people that, if left unattended for days, weeks, or months, poisons
love and greatly weakens the marriage. Anger is not destructive if it is resolved quickly. If a couple can create a safe atmosphere in which to address the concerns and origins of their
anger, then they can enter into the last two deepest levels of intimacy and discover a stronger, more loving marriage.

With the ever-present threat of unresolved, unhealthy, destructive conflict lifted, you will be amazed at how much easier
it is to share your opinions, concerns, expectations, and personal goals with your mate. Practice the upcoming three skills
with your mate daily. When conflict occurs—and it certainly
will—stop, cool down, analyze its true origins, and move forward in your conversation. Remember: each of your is unique
and special, with a set of differences that can drive you apart
or bring you together. Your mate deserves to know you completely, just as you deserve to truly know your mate. Imagine
the joy of feeling safe enough to share your deepest feelings
and needs in a safe and honoring mental environment and
being accepted and treasured for who you are. I've seen it happen to couples the world over—and it can happen to you, too.

In the next three chapters, you will learn the three basic
skills—honor, drive-through listening, and recharging your
mate's "battery" through love—that can blast you through the
wall and into the deepest and most satisfying level of love. All
you need are these skills to propel you beyond the wall of conflict and into the world of true and lasting intimacy. I'm not
implying that your life will turn into one big rose garden.
Spending twenty-four hours of each day sharing feelings and
needs is not our goal. But I can guarantee this: you'll never re-

turn to the emotional prison of strictly speaking in clichés and facts once you experience the wonders behind the wall.

Embracing Conflict as an Opportunity and Moving Toward Deeper Intimacy

What is the secret to handling conflict? You must learn to view conflict as an *opportunity* to be embraced instead of a confrontation to be avoided. The first step is to lay down your emotional armor, the "I'm right, you're wrong" determination, the "my way or the highway" mind-set. See conflict as a tool for digging deeper, not as an untouchable to avoid, flee, or blindly detonate.

Partners in fulfilling relationships have learned to deal effectively with arguments. They have learned that conflict is inevitable and that hiding, avoiding, or denying it only makes it grow. They've learned to identify the fight-or-flight reflex to confrontation and to stop, cool down, and analyze their actions and words. They don't see every confrontation as an attack, merely as an opportunity from which to grow.

This new way of viewing conflict may take a complete reprogramming of your confrontational reflexes. Here's how you can do it.

1. Consider the issues in your life that you and your mate face every day: money, your children, communication, sex, your relatives, time management, work, maintaining your home. Think about these and other constants in your life. These issues are not yours alone. You face them with your mate, and often, these are the issues that reveal your differences and place you in the different types of conflict.

2. Now, think of these daily conflicts as doors. There is a door for each of the issues that arises in your life with your mate. As is the case with a regular door, you can either bang your head against it or spend the time and effort to turn the knob and walk through. Now, you might be thinking, "Gary,

during an argument, the only door I'm looking for is the one marked *exit*." If you will look at each of these issues as an opportunity, not an obstacle, for deeper intimacy with your partner, you will be able to make your relationship deeper and more satisfying every day.

> *I told her when we got married, 'I won't try to change you and you don't try to change me. We agreed that people don't change that way. We also agreed that we'd take turns being mad. I suggested that if we were both mad at the same time, it would be more difficult. We may disagree, but basically we respect what each other wants. . . . I know it may sound ridiculous, but I can get a lot of pleasure out of trading off ideas together and seeing if we can't pull a problem apart and look at it more thoroughly. She's got some very good ideas that I might not think of, and I have some good ideas, too. . . . Ours is a learning relationships that gets better as we learn more.*

> —Keith, happily married over thirty years,
> quoted in American Couples *by Philip Blumstein*
> *and Pepper Schwartz*

Anatomy of an Argument: The Four Stages of Conflict

Before I explain the three skills that will move you into the deepest levels of intimacy and allow you to avoid the four main divorce patterns, I want to show you the "anatomy" of a typical argument. When you see conflict broken down into its key elements, you will find it easier to control and use in your favor. It's important for you to see conflicts for what they are and why they can so easily creep into, and wreak havoc on, your relationship.

In his book *How to Bring Out the Best in Your Spouse*, co-authored by Norman Wright, my friend and colleague Dr. Gary Oliver establishes what he calls the "four stages of conflict": (1) acceptable differences, (2) uncomfortable differences, (3) hitting the wall of conflict, and (4) breaking through the wall of conflict. In reviewing these stages, I can immediately see that they are an integral part of moving a couple to the two deepest levels of intimacy.

The Facts About Differences

"You complete me," said Tom Cruise's character in the movie *Jerry Maguire*. It was an elegant way of expressing the essence of what attracts men and women—their differences. Differences were what made Jerry Maguire and his partner, Dorothy, "whole"—not what each of them already had, but the pieces they lacked that they found in each other. Those pieces "completed" them. But three-quarters of the movie was a testament to how their differences had the power to drive Jerry and Dorothy apart.

It's true that it was your differences that first attracted you and your mate to each other. You were seeking "completion," not separateness, and your differences are the pieces that can make your psychological puzzle complete. We've all heard about the attraction of opposites. Well, it's no fallacy. Differences are attractive, especially in the beginning.

If your wedding officiator had stopped your wedding ceremony and asked, "You say you love each other, but what is it specifically that you see in one another?" you probably would have started with a list of your differences. Maybe you're introverted and your mate is extroverted. Maybe you grew up in a small, close-knit family, always yearning for the camaraderie and community of a big, rollicking clan, which your mate delivered. Maybe you always follow the rules in life, never even dare to jaywalk, and don't tear the "do-not-remove-under-penalty-of-law" inspection sticker off a pillow, while your mate is a renegade, not afraid to test life's boundaries.

Take a moment to recognize your differences. They generally come in two varieties: universal and specific.

• *Universal differences.* There are, first and foremost, the universal gender differences between you and your mate. First there are the obvious physical differences, but that's just the beginning. Let's consider just a few of the psychological differences between the genders. Men love to share facts; women love to express feelings. Men tend to be independent; women tend to be interdependent. Men connect by doing things; women connect by talking. Intimacy, for a woman, means talking and touching; for many men, intimacy represents the simple act of being together, even if it's in front of a television set. Men tend to compete; women tend to cooperate. What are the universal gender differences most evident in your relationship? Write them down! Your partner may be just the opposite of the majority! It's up to you to discover the facts.

• *Specific differences.* Gender differences are only the tip of the iceberg. You and your mate also share infinite differences unique to you as individuals: differences in philosophy, family, genetics, personality, birth order, hometowns, tastes in everything from food to fashion to political opinions. What are your specific differences with your mate? Are you a spender and your mate a saver? Are you a talker and your mate a mute? Are you a trendy clotheshorse and your mate a hapless victim of fashion? Recognize your differences and write them down!

Differences are what initially drew me to my wife, Norma. There I was, a ball of energy and good intentions frequently spinning out of control, and into my life walks this amazing set of differences named Norma. She was so sparky, so enthusiastic, so excited about everything. Her inherent excitement for life literally blazed like a bonfire in her eyes. When I called her on the phone, she'd practically scream, "Oh, hi, Gary!"

It won me over: *this woman really liked me!* At that point, I was sort of breaking the speed limits in my life, "driving haphazardly," you might say, through college. I wasn't dependable; I had a hard time getting things done because I always let them slide until the last minute. Norma impressed me because she could plan, she attended to details, *she got things done.* She was concerned with truth, right and wrong, justice. For me, someone who had been raised in a home without rules, she provided a much-needed sense of calm and order.

She completed me. But here's Norma's take on our differences, which of course is diametrically different from mine:

> One of the main differences between us, something I really admired about Gary, was his desire to help people. I had some of that desire too, but not on that big of a scale. He's also more extroverted than I am. He likes a large group of people. At a party, he says hello to everyone in the room, but most of it's very surface talk. I talk to one person and get to know them deeply. Gary has so much more energy than I do. He packs his day full, from meetings to entertainment. I move a lot slower than he does. When we were dating, I thought that was just super, Gary's high energy.

Now, write down the differences that first attracted you to your mate, completing the chart I've begun for you using my own personal example:

Acceptable Differences

Differences	Me	My Mate
Personality type	Greatly extroverted	Less extroverted
Emotional quotient	Excitable	Even-tempered
Organizational skills	Disorganized	Organized
Attitude toward problems	"Whatever it takes!"	"Follow the rules."

Acceptable Versus Uncomfortable Differences

As you can see, you and your mate have infinite differences, some universal, others specific. It was your differences that brought you together; but it can also be your differences that drive you apart. Only when you understand your specific set of differences can you and your mate begin to truly understand conflict. Of course, the issues are what demand your attention and trigger your emotional reflexes. But the conflict you face always comes down to differences and the unmet needs resulting from those differences.

Yes, some of those differences you found so charming in the courtship stage can become grating over time. This is where differences, originally magnets that attract, can become forces that repel. Think about it: all of those things that drew you to your mate—an extroverted personality, a renegade attitude, a capricious style—gradually lose their charm, especially when they come up against your opposite tendencies. And so you find yourself in a slowly escalating march toward the wall of conflict.

This was true for Norma and me. For instance, my desire to help people, a trait that initially had helped Norma fall in love with me, later became a problem for her:

> After we were married a month, Gary's huge desire to help people started bothering me, because I started feeling about sixth or seventh on his list of priorities. I didn't realize when we were dating how his packed schedule, his abundance of goals, would make me feel unimportant to him. Because I didn't live with him before we got married, I didn't understand the way it would make me feel later. I had made excuses when we were dating because I was so crazy about him. When we got married, it really started hurting deeply. I knew something was very wrong. If he had continued to keep me so far down on his priority list, it would have been so difficult to have stayed in the relationship. I warn couples now that if they have something that irritates them when they are dating, they must be prepared for it to be ten times worse after they get married!

Whew! Obviously, Norma had some concerns that we should have addressed soon after our marriage. Our difference in our daily priorities, so charming in our courtship, became destructive in our marriage because it made Norma feel like she was not the most important, or even the second-most important, thing in my daily schedule. I never realized any of this hurt because she rarely spoke up about it. If she said anything at all, it was so loving and soft-spoken I missed its meaning completely. But that was secondary to an even greater difference, which still plagues our relationship today: our difference in attitudes about following rules.

Norma and I love to visit Silver Dollar City, voted this year as the number one amusement park in the world, and it's practically right in our backyard, near Branson, Missouri. The only problem is that everyone else loves to visit Silver Dollar City, too. So, typically running late because of my "pack-everything-into-a-day" schedule, we find ourselves facing the park's perpetually tangled parking lot. Determined to make it to a show on time, I am typically in no mood to search for a parking space.

Luckily, about five years ago, the owners of the park had invited us for dinner, graciously extending the one-time invitation to park in the Silver Dollar City employee parking lot. A new world opened to me. The employee lot also comes with a shortcut to enter the park itself and it's a million times more convenient than fighting the crowds in the regular parking lot. So ever since that dinner, when we approach the park, I can't help myself!—I head for the employee parking lot.

"You can't park here," my wife Norma always says to me, ever the rule-follower, nodding toward the sign proclaiming, "Read the sign, Gary, 'Employees Only. Please post your pass in car window.' "

She had once admired my maverick, high-energy style of getting tasks done. That was one difference that defined us. But now, after thirty-six years of marriage, it's a difference that has become uncomfortable for both of us at times. Norma is a woman who *always* follows the rules; I am a man for whom rules were made to be bent or—if basically legal, socially acceptable, and convenient to my cause at hand—broken. So I look around the lot, and while other cars are there, it is usually by no means full. We are usually late and we need to get into the park. I'm thinking, "We've parked here once before, so why can't we park here again?"

"Why can't I park here?" I ask Norma, playing out my difference as the maverick, the rule breaker, the role that originally attracted my wife to me and is ingrained in my character.

"Because it says so, Gary, right there," she'll answer, sticking to her role as the straight arrow, the rule follower, the difference that originally attracted me to her and equally ingrained in her character.

So the inherent difference that brought us together in the beginning—my maverick spirit, her adherence to rules and order—is now not only uncomfortable, it's taking us closer and closer toward the wall of conflict.

Now, take a moment to write down your own "uncomfortable differences."

Uncomfortable Differences

Differences	My Style	Mate's Style	My Feelings
Spirit	Renegade	Rule follower	She's too stuck on rules and details.
Personality	Extroverted	Less extroverted	She hides her feelings sometimes
Financial style	Saver	Spender	I can't make enough to support her spending!
Emotional style	Excitable	Calm, but nervous	Why is she so worried about everything?

Hitting the Wall of Conflict

Once an opinion is expressed, you can't take it back. It has a momentum of its own, carrying you toward the wall. Assaulting all of your senses, overheating your emotions, the escalating opinions will eventually try to convince you that it's easier to abdicate from reason than to analyze the sources. So you're sentenced to repeat the cycle over and over again, doing that crazy dance. Here, once again, are the three steps:

• *Critical remarks.* One critical remark begins the dance. Unable to reconcile their differences, one or both partner berates the other: "Look what you did!" "Why are you so impractical?" "Look how much you spent!" The journey toward intimacy stops and the verbal jousting begins. "You're not a person of integrity!"

• *Condescending comments.* This escalates the tension of the critical remarks—and, believe me, this step hurts. Bam, bam, bam!—the words land like blows. "Why can't you ever do anything right?" "Why can't you ever be on time?" "You're just like your mother/father/sister/brother!"

• *Return to seemingly safer levels.* Conflict is painful, so one partner—or both—abdicates, retreating from conflict, returning to the safer levels of superficiality, speaking in clichés and sharing facts. In these shallow levels, a couple can languish for days, months, years, or decades before the dance begins anew.

In our recurring parking drama, Norma feels uncomfortable parking in an "illegal" space. She has shared her opinion with me: "Because it says so, Gary, right there!" What she really means is this: "You know it's important to me that we follow the rules in life." But because of our inherent differences, I cannot simply accept her opinion and move on. In the simple act of pointing out our difference of opinion, she has unknowingly hit a realert button in my psyche. She has made me feel that my values, my belief system, is threatened. I feel vulnerable, exposed. I feel defensive, and therefore, I do not retreat. I counterattack. I challenge! I'm capable of escalating the conversation into a full-blown argument.

"Why are you so worried about little details?" I snap, pulling into the parking spot and propelling us face-to-face with the wall of conflict.

"Because I think it's important to obey the rules," she replies, in a tone that tells me I'm ruining a perfectly lovely evening before it's even begun.

My wife is showing me an integral part of the ultimate re-

118 • GARY SMALLEY

lationship roadmap—her unique feelings and needs, the stuff of which the two deepest levels of intimacy are made. But I can't hear her, much less follow her desires. I'm getting angry! We have both expressed an opinion, but I don't like the opinion she's expressed. I think that she has challenged my role not merely as the designated driver and car parker but also as a man, husband, provider. She has challenged what I see as my responsibility to get us to our appointment on time, no matter what it takes! My rising level of anger and frustration clouds my judgment. In this state, I don't want to analyze or even discuss the situation. My initial reflex is simply to *win*.

"Sure, there are rules, but we've parked here before," I'll say. "We aren't bothering anybody, are we? Do you think we're in anybody's way? Don't forget that the owners told us that we could park here."

Notice my tone: critical, bordering on condescension. I'm trying to protect myself and my vulnerability, but I'm too scared and stubborn to admit that. It's not easy to blurt out the truth: "Honey, don't you see that I have to belittle you and ignore your opinion and park in this outlaw parking place to defend my side, opinion, my own value?" Still, internally I'm almost bleating out my plea: "I know Norma's right, but I can't be wrong and still be a man!"

"I think you should look for another place," she insists, not giving an inch. "No one ever said you could park here anytime you want. They didn't give you an employee pass."

"Okay, so I'll ask for a letter for the next time," I snap in a sarcastic tone. "Will that satisfy you?"

But the only place I move is even closer to the wall. My stand—that there is no problem in parking in the restricted lot—has become a red-hot issue, a difference to defend. And so I move to the next level of the dance of conflict—condescension—shaking my finger at my beloved and employing the warring language of overgeneralization: "You always . . . !" "You never . . . !" "You're just like your mother/father/sister/brother!"

"You always just do whatever the signs say, huh?" I bark. "You can't think for yourself, I guess."

We can always find the flaws in our mate during an argument, can't we?

"Yes, I can think for myself," she says, joining me in the mud pit that conflict lays down for you to wrestle in. "I'm thinking about the time you broke the law by driving on the shoulder because of the traffic jam."

Then, it all falls down on me like a crate of rotten eggs: pain, disappointment, humiliation. "Oh, why did I bring up this parking stuff when I know how she feels?" I think to myself. But now it's much too late. I can't turn to her and say, "Honey, why are we arguing about such a trivial matter as parking a car?" My ego won't let me admit defeat and she is too upset with my behavior to lead me in the direction that she inherently knows we have to go, into to the deeper levels of intimacy.

I can just imagine what some of you are thinking: What does Gary do? Does he pull out of the employees' parking lot and do what would make Norma happier? If not, how can he use this conflict to deepen his love and intimacy? Good question. Because, if I'm intent on banging my head against the wall of conflict, my thinking will go something like this: If I lose this argument, Norma will win in other, less trivial areas of our life. I reason that if I hold my ground in the parking issue, I will have drawn a line in the sand that would say, "Do not try to control me, I need to maintain my independence and my uniqueness." And what a blind fool I will have become. Because during a heated argument, I—like most human beings—cannot see the door that could take my wife and me into the deeper levels of love and understanding. I just see "red," I think only of myself, and I allow my emotions to drive me back to the shallow levels of intimacy, to that place where temporarily there is no conflict, no pain, no vulnerability . . . and no hope of growth or intimacy.

What can you do in a situation like this? How do you create a win-win situation when a full-blown conflict is underway?

Well, I could have honored her and said, "Okay, it's no big deal," and then moved the car and retreated to the temporary safety of speaking in clichés and sharing facts. But that's merely prolonging the conflict, not using it to deepen understanding.

There is, however, hope ahead. Let's begin by recalling an argument that took you and your mate to the wall of conflict.

Take an incident and break it down into its individual steps, using my example as a template.

Hitting the Wall: A Breakdown of Events

The Issue	Apparent Conflict	Hidden Conflict
Where to park the car	Whether or not to break the official rules	Getting to the show on time
Expressing opinions, concerns, and expectations	*Me:* "It's not hurting anybody and we've done it before." *Her:* "All rules are on the level, and we should obey them."	*Me:* "I will do what it takes to get us there on time." *Her:* "It is more important to obey the rules than to take an easy way out."
Critical remarks	*Me:* "Why are you so stuck on details when it's not a big issue?" *Her:* "Why can't you do what you are supposed to?"	*Me:* "I will feel guilty if we don't get to the show on time. It will be my fault." *Her:* "I don't want my car to get impounded!"
Condescension	*Me:* "You can't think for yourself." *Her:* "You're a law breaker."	*Me:* "Now I feel guilty for being late and for suggesting that we break laws." *Her:* "This is embarrassing to me. It's as if he is saying, 'I'm Gary Smalley, I can park wherever I want!' I find that mortifying!"
Retreat to safer place	*Me:* "Whatever. It's not a big deal anyway." *Her:* "Just do what you want."	*Me:* "I don't want her angry and steaming all night about this." *Her:* "I can't get through to him."

Now, ask yourself: What could you or your mate have done differently that would have stopped the argument from escalating? What could he or she have said to make me feel more comfortable in sharing my true feelings and needs? What could I have said to do the same for him or her?

What would have allowed you both to share opinions and move through conflict and into the deeper levels of intimacy? For my wife and me, the answer was amazingly simple: We could have agreed to never allow ourselves to hurt each other out of anger. We could have agreed that we would never surrender our individual ideologies, but would simply stop talking when were in conflict, until our anger subsides. We could have decided to address the issue later in a very organized and profoundly simple way that would really work. In the meantime, we would *listen* without reacting and drop or change the subject as soon as we could. Now that I realize these important things, I can surrender my armor. I know that it is important to her for me to obey the rules. It would be such an easy thing for me to accomplish merely by consistently parking in legal spaces. But that type of thinking doesn't benefit both of us as a team. She's important and so am I. When you're banging your heads against the wall of conflict, the anger is all you can see. Your mind begins to play tricks on you. You forget that you've been to this wall before and couldn't break through. After all, who wouldn't grow discouraged and frustrated? And so you revert to where your anger has already taken you, clichés and facts, instead of moving forward.

Breaking Through the Wall: Understanding, Growth, and Resolution of Conflict

In the traditional stages of an argument—origination, escalation, and abandonment—few couples will successfully even be able to see the door within the wall of conflict, much less open it up and walk through it. You will see how to break through the wall in later chapters, using the most powerful techniques in modern relationship science. Going to the deeper levels— the destination of the ultimate relationship roadmap—is easier than you think. But staying there is next to impossible unless you understand the science of conflict. Before we go to the solution, you first must fully understand the problem.

Now that you have identified the land mines of conflict— your differences—it's time to defuse them. First, you must understand that our inherent differences keep us from being able to see and recognize our partners' understandings and feelings. You're banging your head against the wall because somebody's *feelings* aren't being understood and somebody's *needs* aren't being met. That's it! It's just that simple. In order to find the door in the wall of conflict and walk through it together with your mate, you must first realize what it is hiding.

In preparing this book, we surveyed more than 3,000 married couples over the course of a year, discovering that there are basic reasons why couples argue. Each of the reasons was tied to an unmet need in one or both of the partners. In the next several chapters, I will show you how you can use the three skills of optimum relationships—honor, drive-through listening, and recharging your mate's "needs battery" through love—to address these crucial human needs that must be met within yourself and your mate. Conflicts are inevitable, but learning to fulfill your mate's needs can help you stave off the most destructive variety of conflict—that resulting from unmet needs—before it can weaken your marriage. Using the three skills, you will be able to eliminate this danger and achieve the deepest levels of intimacy and the greatest satisfaction in your relationship.

Now let's step through the door, through the wall of conflict, and get to work.

CHAPTER FIVE

Honor: The First and Foremost Skill

Skill Number 1

Honor

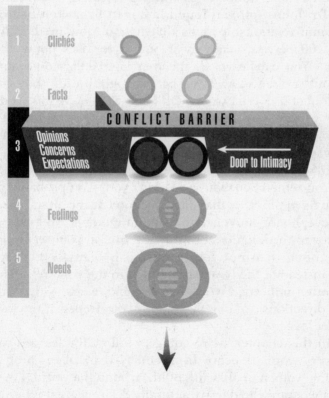

1 Clichés

2 Facts

CONFLICT BARRIER

3 Opinions
Concerns
Expectations

Door to Intimacy

4 Feelings

5 Needs

I'M ASSUMING THAT you're now willing to step out of the emotionally cold and intellectually devoid world of speaking in clichés and facts. I hope you're willing to lay down your emotional armor, to view conflict as an opportunity to be explored instead of an obstacle to be avoided. But most likely you're staring up at what may seem like an incredibly daunting wall of conflict, separating you from the deeper levels of intimacy, and you might be thinking, "How can I break through? Is there a key or a password to actually enjoy deeper intimacy?"

Well, the simple yet incredibly powerful principle of optimum relationships can summed up in a single majestic word: *honor*. **Honor opens the door to the fourth and fifth levels of intimacy.** And it's a master key. No loving relationship ever lasts without it. It's become such a precept in relationship science that virtually every marriage expert seems to be saying the same thing: honor, or else! In his research, relationship expert Dr. John Gottman found honor to be such a bedrock of optimum relationship skills that he can now predict divorce with 100 percent accuracy if one mate loses honor for the other. "You can learn all the marriage skills you want, but without reverence, awe, respect, and admiration (other terms for honor) it doesn't work." Dr. Scott Stanley writes, "I do not know of any long term loving relationship that doesn't have honor. Honor is like gasoline to relationship. The lower your fuel gauge, the less satisfying your relationship will be."

HONOR.

You remember that word, don't you? You probably said it in the form of a vow that day you stood at the altar, repeating, "To love, honor, and cherish." In that moment, you were given the key to the kingdom of intimacy. But on your wedding day, more often than not your attention is focused on the word *love,* instead of the two that follow it in the vow. Yet it is those two often unheeded words—*honor* and *cherish*—that are virtual directions to the destination of deeper intimacy and deeper love.

In this chapter, we're going to follow the lessons written on every woman's heart. In my thirty years of research interviewing women in all walks of life around the world, I've never met a woman who doesn't naturally desire a great relationship and instinctively know what it takes to get there. As I've noted, whenever I ask questions about what a great relationship represents, communication is always at the top of the list. Inherent in communication is honor. Even in the darkest situations, when hope seems to be gone, honor can restore what once was lost. In this chapter you're going to learn how to use the skill of *honor* to pass through the wall that separates the superficial from the profound in relationships.

You're going to learn to use honor to create nothing short of a breakthrough in your relationship, which is, after all, the word, the experience, for which I know you have been waiting. You're ready for a breakthrough, right? You've read a long way already—and you're ready to get behind that wall and finally see that world I've been discussing and describing! You didn't buy this book for a lecture. You bought it for a promise. Your purchase was like buying a ticket, and the destination was intimate communication, real intimacy—not a little shake on the shoulder or a gentle stirring of intellectual brain cells, but a really earth-shattering emotional earthquake. You wanted a breakthrough so real and inarguable that you and your mate would look at each other and wonder how you lived without it.

That type of breakthrough is within your reach! The skills I will discuss in the next three chapters—honor, drive-through listening, and recharging your mate's "needs battery" through love—will help you break through the wall of conflict and reach the deepest levels of intimacy. These three skills are a culmination of my life's work, the most effective route to deeper love I've yet encountered. Once mastered, these skills can lead you to your breakthrough. Again, these skills aren't the only ones employed in great relationships; they're the ones to start with and, for many couples, they'll be all that's needed to get to the promised land of optimum relationships.

What Is Honor?

In my thirty years of research, the word *honor* has been such a recurring theme—in both my studies and my interviews with couples—that I've practically devoted my life to its study. In each of my thirteen books I have exhaustively examined honor as a skill to get to the deepest levels of intimacy. But it occurred to me this year that I've never detailed the practical steps for *how* to honor. In this chapter, I'd like to do exactly that: to show you how to use honor, the most powerful of the three skills of optimum relationships, to send your relationship to the deepest levels of intimacy.

There are three main steps to conveying honor:

1. The decision to honor your mate
2. Listing honorable attributes
3. Proclaiming the list and lifting it up for all to see

When you finish reading this chapter—in which material about the critical importance of "deciding" to honor your mate constitutes three-quarters, and the "how-to-honor" sections one-quarter—you'll understand that once you decide to honor, the how-to honor becomes almost second nature. First comes the all-important decision to honor, then you'll know how.

Let's examine these steps one at a time.

The First Act of Honor: The Decision

Honor is, first and foremost, a decision. It is the simple decision to place high value, worth, and importance on another person, to view him or her as a priceless gift and grant that person a position in your life worthy of great respect. Love involves putting that decision into action. In other words, honor is a gift we give to others. It isn't purchased by their actions or contingent on our emotions. You're giving them distinction whether or not they like it, want it, or deserve it. It's a *conferring distinction,* much like an honorary degree. You give honor to a loved one merely because that person is alive and breathing, not because he or she has done something to deserve it. You just do it; it's a decision *you* make. You will soon see how honoring your mate gives legs to the words "I love you." It puts that statement into action.

Remember the dentist and his wife, the couple with the unspoken agreement to communicate only in facts? Remember how their relationship descended into banality and despair, to the point where the wife became so fed up she had her bags packed in the hallway and her mind set on leaving? "I was always trying to get his attention: trying to be a part of what he was doing: barbecuing for the church, going from this meeting to that meeting, signing up for this committee and that committee," she remembers. "I was trying to control him, to get into his life. I thought he did too much and didn't spend enough time with us. Finally, I had enough."

It was only when she could put her frustration into a word picture that he could understand—that she saw the state of her relationship as like a dental infection that was so close to her heart it was about to kill her. Could she awaken her emotionally absent husband from his self-imposed stupor and see things as they really were? Yes, but it wasn't until he made a conscious *decision* to honor his wife and his family—above all the myriad activities he had spent so long honoring—that his relationship began to change. Even then, his wife doubted him, thinking his words empty promises. But he showed her that he truly loved her, not by giving her material things but by bestowing upon her the greatest gift one person can give another: honor.

Honor is not only the first step of love, it's also the single most important principle for building an intimate relationship. The literal definition of honor is "To give preference to someone by attaching high value to them." When you confer honor you're thinking, "I'm married to an extremely valuable person. I'm making the decision to consider him or her even more important than I consider myself to be." Honor is the goal, the prize, the hope that you bestow upon your mate. No one ever reaches perfection, but that hope is always before you; it both guides your relationship and regulates it. I've found that honor can be a reminder; it makes me want to repair any damage I cause in my relationship, simply because I honor my mate. It's like a neon sign flashing before me, re-minding me to make my actions, words, and deeds as honor-ing as they can be. When I make a mistake—and, of course, we all do—my sense of honor redirects me back to the base of my love, which is in essence acting toward my mate in honor-ing ways.

Once you commit to honoring your mate and your rela-tionship above all else, you are essentially searching for a door through that wall of conflict with the key of honor in your hand. When you understand and practice honor, you are able to not only recognize the door but open it. Despite your differ-ences and the conflicts to which your differences can lead, honor can take you to the deeper levels of intimacy.

Honor isn't merely important to relationships, it's ab-solutely critical. Without honor, you cannot attain intimacy in a relationship; moreover, it is impossible to create even a *functional* relationship without honor. Honor has to be the center of the relationship, and it is not a difficult strength to master and practice. Once you make the conscious decision to honor your mate, above all else on earth, you will see how simple it can be. All it takes in the beginning is a decision, one that you must make now. The first act toward getting honor into your relationship is deciding that your mate is important.

In her landmark book *You Just Don't Understand,* Deborah Tannen discusses what women really want. In reading it, I could see the signposts of the ultimate relationship roadmap. Here's an important passage: "In discussing her novel *The Tem-ple of My Familiar,* Alice Walker explained that a woman in the novel falls in love with a man because she sees him as 'a giant ear,' " writes Tannen. "Walker went on to remark that although people may think that they are falling in love because of sexual attraction or some other force, 'really what we are looking for is someone to be able to hear us.' . . . We all want above all to be heard—but not merely to be heard. We want our words to be valued, to be understood—heard for what we think we are saying, for what we know we meant. With increased under-standing of the ways women and men use language should come a decrease in frequency of the complaint, 'You just don't understand.' "

A giant ear. That's the essence of honor: the ability to listen, with ears and eyes that reflect the tremendous value we attach to our mates, the ability to listen without anger, and to take action on what we've heard. That's the direction in which the roadmap points: not toward money, career success, or material possessions, but to the simple, absolutely free and simple act of listening and understanding someone who is immensely valuable. It is not in a woman's true nature to be dishonored, dispirited, despondent, or dismissed. She yearns for—and stands ever-ready to bestow—honor. Once you realize this is the primary direction of the ultimate relationship roadmap, you can begin to employ honor as a tool to blast through the wall of conflict and reach the two deepest levels of intimacy. Because of your honor, you and your mate will feel safe to be who you are and to say what you are in an atmosphere of honor.

But we are conditioned to believe just the opposite—and the early years of my marriage bore the weight of that mistake in judgment. At the beginning of my marriage to Norma, I stubbornly believed I was on my way to becoming the husband of her dreams: a strong personality, a successful businessman, an able provider. My ears were closed—and, thus, so was my ability to convey honor—until I made a conscious decision to honor my wife above all earthly things.

That single decision took me to the destination of the ultimate relationship roadmap: true and lasting intimacy with my wife.

To the Undecided Spouse: Honor or Else!

Mates who have not yet decided to honor are not hard to recognize, except to themselves. They're the husbands or wives in such deep denial that only when their spouse's bags are packed and sitting in the hall will they wake up and realize what's been happening in their own home. I know the scenario well; it almost happened to me. If you had stopped me on the street and asked me if I was living up to my marriage vow—to love, honor, and cherish my wife—I would have said, "Of course!" But I was honoring a dozen extraneous things before her. Yes, I loved my wife, but I didn't know the critical importance of *honoring* her. I didn't give her priority status. Instead, I unconsciously gave a dozen other factors —work, sports, community activities—foremost preference through my actions, words, and deeds. Yes, the "wanna-be" relationship expert was a relational invalid—until I learned to honor.

Consider the newlywed Smalleys on their first Valentine's Day together, thirty-five years ago. Norma, who at that time was working as a schoolteacher, had planned an elaborate first Valentine's Day celebration for us. She had never cooked a roast beef dinner before, but she would learn for this enchanted evening, for which she also had turned our small dining room into a romantic harbor with a new tablecloth, candles, cardboard hearts, the works.

Most men would have been alert to the fact that it was Valentine's Day from billboards, commercials, and card displays in stores. Not me. I had no idea. I had prepared nothing. I phoned home around two in the afternoon. "Hey, Hon," I said, "I have a basketball game tonight at the college. I'm playing at six tonight. Will you come and watch?"

There was dead silence on the other end of the phone. "Do you know what day this is?" she asked me quietly.

"Uh . . . no."

"It's Valentine's Day, and I've cooked you a special dinner," she said. "I've been working on it all day."

I knew I was in trouble, but I couldn't miss the game! I blurted out my first reaction without thinking, much less listening, protecting *my* desires and *my* agenda. I made a dishonoring statement that continues to haunt me thirty-five years later. "I promised the guys I would be there," I said. "They don't have enough players without me. Just leave the dinner the way it is, and we can finish cooking when I get home tonight!"

Those words make me cringe today. I can't remember how she replied to that absolutely dishonoring response, but somehow I thought that everything was fine when we hung up. I got home around 8:45 that night. Norma hadn't come to the game.

"Hey, honey, guess what?!" I shouted, bounding into the kitchen. "We won! Isn't that great?"

No response from Norma.

I looked around. The air was heady with the scent of roast beef, but the dining room was dark and silent. "What's for dinner?" I asked her. She turned away and said nothing.

Then, I saw the cold roast beef and the melted candles and the now-forlorn cardboard hearts. Laid out cold and dark on that table sat my relationship with my wife, a woman who naturally honored me, a woman who had worked all day to show me her love and honor, a woman to whom honor was as natural an act as breathing. Norma, like women the world over, naturally understood that relationships involve ceremony—decorations, candles, Valentine's Day cards, and sentiments—not merely subsistence.

"Can't we just warm it up?" I asked her.

I had ruined her Valentine's Day, but worse I had dishonored her. I had shown her through my actions that I honored my basketball game more than the most sacred day of love. Thirty-five years later, Norma cannot even think about that Valentine's Day without feeling some sickness in her stomach. It took a lot of work—and a lot of learning about priorities and how to honor my mate—to repair the damage I did that day, and kept doing for the first years of my marriage. I didn't realize it then, but many of the things I was doing not only dishonored Norma but dishonored our marriage.

For a few years we bounced back and forth off the wall of conflict. Norma kept hoping that I'd see the light, but gradually that hope began dying. She saw her dream for a totally fulfilling and honoring marriage—the destination on the ultimate relationship roadmap—slipping away. I suppose she began expressing her feelings and needs through inner talking, because I wasn't emotionally or physically there for her. Then, about five years into our marriage, I walked into the living room after another long day at the office, shouting my usual, "Hi,

Hon, I'm home!" and the results of five years of befuddled bouncing on and off that wall of conflict smacked me right in the face.

I thought love was a game and, like most games, force was the only way to win it. How wrong I was! People have to remain true to themselves and they have to be respected for their differences, their individuality. But, of course, I didn't know that. I had spent the beginning years of my marriage incessantly trying to convince Norma that my opinions, my differences, were superior to hers. Because she loved me, and because she sought to avoid conflict, she tried to see things my way. Gradually, Norma turned sullen. She lost her spirit, her sparkle. She suffered bouts of depression and stiffened as far as responding in a loving manner. She turned cold at times. By trying to change her, I ended up literally suffocating her true nature. I lost what I loved most about my mate: her individuality, her sparkle, the differences that made Norma unique.

I hadn't noticed it until one night, when Norma's simple response to my nightly, "Hi, Hon, I'm home!" quickly commanded my attention. Dr. Gary Oliver recently told me that anytime one person controls another to the point where that controlled person doesn't even know who he or she is anymore creates a recipe for disaster. Maybe they seem satisfied and quiet and meek, but it's only a temporary lull. Within five years he or she will come uncorked. On the day this happened to Norma, I bounded into our living room, with my nightly, "Hi, Hon!" and she let me know that she had finally had enough.

She *ignored* my arrival. The look on her face should have tipped me off to the weight she was under, the baggage she was bearing. But I still couldn't see it. I asked her to tell me what was bothering her and, finally, she told me the flat-out, soul-shaking truth, the same truth that rattled the dentist in my hometown, the one who honored everything in his world before his spouse:

"Gary, I feel that everything on this earth is far more important to you than I am," Norma told me.

Then, she unleashed a litany of things she believed I preferred to her: my counseling practice, football games, television, the newspaper, my friends, hobbies, extracurricular activities. "Gary, I can spend hours working in the kitchen, and you never say a word of thanks," she said. "I can farm out the kids to a baby-sitter and have a candlelit dinner all prepared for you, and the phone will ring and you'll answer it and say, 'Oh, I'm not doing anything important—just eating dinner. Sure, I'll be right over.' Then, you're gone, telling me to keep dinner warm for you in the oven."

That awakened me. There I was, trying to be a relationship expert, advising couples on how to create optimum relationships, when my own marriage was in steady decay. Suddenly, I felt exhausted. I literally collapsed into a chair.

"Honey, what do you think is wrong in our relationship?" I asked.

She drew back from me, her eyes welling. "Oh, no," she said. "You're not going to get me to share what I'm feeling and then turn it into another lecture on what I'm doing wrong."

I lowered my voice and practically begged her to tell me. I promised not to lecture but to finally listen. She eventually opened up her heart to me and aired the painful truth about how my actions had hurt her. And while she had told me these things a hundred times before, on this day they sunk into my brain. I listened, really listened, and it changed my life. I made a commitment, a vow, that I carry on to this day: I would place my wife above all else on this earth and I would show her my honor, my commitment, through my words, actions, and deeds every day.

At the moment of that decision and declaration, I discovered the raw power of honor. But recognizing the word alone was not enough. I had to *decide* to honor her, and to *show* that decision in my words, actions, and deeds. I didn't realize it at the time, but now I see what happened. As a team, we began to raise each other's value. From that point forward, our words and actions toward each other changed. We still argue, we still do hurtful things to each other, but now the things we do are mere temporary storms—because our honor is permanent. It's the foundation of our relationship. Every time we make a mistake, or goof up like everyone does, we follow the bright light of honor back to the core—our loving relationship.

Honor in Action:
Honoring Your Differences

Honoring your mate's similarities—the things you have in common—is easy. But that alone does not constitute honor. Honor is the act of recognizing, respecting, and loving your mate's differences.

Let me paint you a word picture: Think of the deepest levels of intimacy as a room, a big, spacious room, where your mate keeps their hopes, dreams, and aspirations, a place that exists deep within all of us where our feelings and needs reside. Think of it as your childhood bedroom, that favorite, private world where all of your possessions were posted on the wall and littered around the floor, the place you lived in so completely that you could define yourself by its contents.

It's the place you call home.

When you had friends over to your house as a child, your first words on their arrival were most likely, "Let's go to my room!" You were saying more than that, of course. You were saying, "Come into my world and let me show you who I am." Children enter each other's rooms with a sense of wonder and discovery, honoring the differences that are as apparent as their toys and posters and photographs, and couples in the first stages of courtship tend to offer the keys to each other's rooms freely. Think back to when you and your mate were dating. You were constantly honoring your date, always ready to show that person your dreams, your desires. In courtship, men, especially, seek to learn about women. In their mission of winning the woman, they listen, honor, and cherish—they can talk for hours on the phone.

When women get together with each other, they provide a striking exception to the rule. Women seem to be able to go to each other's "rooms" naturally. Women love nothing better than to visit their friends' homes, to examine the most private corners of their friends and loved ones' lives. They're curious about the differences that define people. You can hear their natural inquisitiveness in their conversation. They're always asking, "Who is in this picture on the wall? What does this mean to you? Where did you get that?"

When mates try to show each other their rooms, however, the process doesn't go as smoothly. Most people take one glimpse of their mate's room and sneak or storm out. Why? Because what they see on the walls of their mates' rooms are what's at the center of every person: differences. It's a room lined with bookshelves, almost like a library or an archive, but instead of a collection of books, the shelves are filled with what makes this person different—values, memories, belief systems, emotional possessions—all of the things that make a mate an individual. For most people, seeing these differences at once is overwhelming. The first reaction is to think or even say, "What is all this stuff? It's certainly not mine! It's not what I grew up with!"

When you make the decision to honor your differences with your mate, you step into another world: your mate's world, your mate's "room." Inside, you'll become privy to their most personal feelings and needs, and you will be fulfilling one of those needs: the need to be honored and valued. Inside that room is the very soul of your mate, and when you step inside, you must validate and honor what you see there if you want to stay inside.

Once you make the decision to honor and validate your mate's differences, you can step inside his or her room. Why? Because you're no longer threatened by the differences that define him or her, differences that once had the power to make you feel like you had to be defensive. By honoring your mate's individual aspects you're not invalidating your own. you're merely opening yourself up to possibility. This is the essence of true intimacy.

I'm asking you to step inside your mate's room now. How? By simply deciding to honor the differences that make that person unique. Once you do this, you'll see that this room is a major destination on the ultimate relationship roadmap. Your mate will feel honored when you take the time and attention to see his or her "room" clearly, secure in the infinite ways that he or she is different from you. You won't want to go in and redecorate your mate's room. Once you reach that point, you and your mate may begin sharing with each other in deeper, more meaningful communication. Then, your mate will feel ready to walk into your room. You feel the honor that comes with having someone in your room who wants to be there, wants to learn about you, wants to know your feelings and needs.

Honor is a powerful force, the virtual foundation of love. Properly deployed it can transcend your daily life and all its pitfalls and take you regularly into the deep levels of intimacy. Remember this: *you don't have to like every aspect of a person to love him or her.* Love is a permanent commitment, invulnerable to every day's temporary likes and dislikes. You are going to be hit with the gale force of minute opinions on various issues on a regular basis, but you must not empower them. Instead, recognize, then honor, the place of those differing opinions—your differences. Too many people are torn apart by the little issues; unprotected and dishonored, their love is destroyed.

Honor Above All . . .

Let me show you another practical way to implement the element of honor in your relationship. A story by inspirational speaker and writer Steven James is called "I'll Never Understand My Wife," and it gets to the heart of the skill of honoring, which is essentially the act of honoring differences between you and your mate. You may not understand all—or even many—of the differences you share with your mate, but if you can accept and honor those differences, you will open the door in your wall.

After their wedding, James writes of how his not understanding his wife—but honoring her nonetheless—has deepened his relationship.

I'll never understand my wife.

The day she moved in with me, she started opening and closing my kitchen cabinets, gasping, "You don't have any shelf paper! We're going to have to get some shelf paper before I move my dishes in."

"But why?" I asked innocently.

"To keep the dishes clean," she answered matter-of-factly. I didn't understand how the dust would magically migrate off the dishes if they had sticky blue paper under them, but I knew when to be quiet.

Then came the day when I left the toilet seat up.

"We never left the toilet seat up in my family," she scolded. "It's impolite."

"It wasn't impolite in my family," I said sheepishly.

"Your family didn't have cats."

In addition to these lessons, I also learned how I was supposed to squeeze the toothpaste tube, which towel to use after a shower and where the spoons are supposed to go when I set the table. I had no idea I was so uneducated.

Nope, I'll never understand my wife.

She alphabetizes her spices, washes dishes before sending them through the dishwasher, and sorts laundry into different piles before throwing them into the washing machine. Can you imagine?

She wears pajamas to bed. I didn't think anyone in North America still wore pajamas to bed. She has a coat that makes her look like Sherlock Holmes. "I could get you a new coat," I offered.

"No. This one was my grandmother's," she said, decisively ending the conversation.

Then, after we had kids, she acted even stranger. Wearing those pajamas all day long, eating breakfast at 1:00 P.M., carrying around a diaper bag the size of a mini-van, talking in one-syllable paragraphs.

She carried our baby everywhere—on her back, on her front, in her arms, over her shoulder. She never set her down, even when other young mothers shook their heads as they set down the car seat with their baby in it, or peered down into their playpens. What an oddity she was, clutching that child.

My wife also chose to nurse her even when her friends told her not to bother. She picked up the baby whenever she cried, even though people told her it was healthy to let her wail.

"It's good for her lungs to cry," they would say.

"It's better for her heart to smile," she'd answer.

One day a friend of mine snickered at the bumper sticker my wife had put on the back of our car: "Being a Stay-at-Home Mom Is a Work of Heart."

"My wife must have put that on there," I said.

"My wife works," he boasted.

"So does mine," I said, smiling.

Once, I was filling out one of those warranty registration cards and I checked "homemaker" for my wife's occupation. Big mistake. She glanced over it and quickly corrected me. "I am not a homemaker. I am not a housewife. I am a mother."

"But there's no category for that," I stammered.

"Add one," she said.

I did.

And then one day, a few years later, she lay in bed smiling when I got up to go to work.

"What's wrong?" I asked.

"Nothing. Everything is wonderful. I didn't have to get up at all last night to calm the kids. And they didn't crawl in bed with us."

"Oh," I said, still not understanding.

"It was the first time I've slept through the night in four years." It was? Four years? That's a long time. I hadn't even noticed. Why hadn't she ever complained? I would have.

One day, in a thoughtless moment, I said something that sent her fleeing to the bedroom in tears. I went in to apologize. She knew I meant it because by then I was crying, too.

"I forgive you," she said. And you know what? She did. She never brought it up again. Not even when she got angry and could have hauled out the heavy artillery. She forgave, and she forgot.

Nope, I'll never understand my wife. And you know

what? Our daughter is acting more and more like her mother every day.

If she turns out to be anything like her mom, someday there's going to be one more lucky guy in the world, thankful for the shelf paper in his cupboard.

Differences. Steven James has detailed a laundry list of how he and his wife are different. But he no longer debates these differences; he simply accepts them, and, in that acceptance, he's learned to honor them.

That's the secret of optimum relationships: to see differences as strengths instead of weaknesses. James's proclamation—that he will never understand his wife and her ways so different from his own—honors his wife in a very profound way. He may never be able to understand her, but he has made a conscious decision to respect, value, and honor her. She makes his life better because of her differences and in spite of them.

She completes him.

And even better, he knows she completes him. He honors her, both by supporting her on a daily basis and through the act of writing, posting, and proclaiming his devotion. You don't have to be a professional writer like Steven James to make such a powerful proclamation. All you have to do is write your own testament to the wonders of your mate. Post and proclaim your love for the person and all the differences—the special qualities—that make him or her your unique and special life partner.

The Decision to Determine Your Mate's "Color"

In my ultimate relationship seminars, I use the analogy of color to teach people about honoring their differences. I tell my students that human beings naturally want to become more intimate in their friendships. They want to share their opinions and be valued; they want to share their concerns and be understood and listened to and valued; they want to talk about their expectations and feel that their expectations are valid. But we have been brought up to believe that true love can only be between two people who think, act, and feel identically as one, instead of understanding the fact that people are individuals, and only when you quit trying to change them, and embrace and honor the differences that make them unique, can true love begin to grow.

To help people see how radically different they can be from their mates, I ask my seminar attendees to see themselves as a unique and brilliant set of colors. In my seminars, I use the colors yellow and blue to represent the two people in a relationship—yellow for women and blue for men, but those are only two of the infinite color combinations you and your mate might be. We are all unique individuals, with our own backgrounds, cultural heritage, racial heritage, parental upbringing, and personal experiences, especially when it comes to relationships. For example, some of us went steady five or six times and broke up every time; some only had one serious relationship. In my theory, there is a unique and special shade of every color in the rainbow for each individual.

Problems arise when people share their opinions and concerns and expectations with their mates. The mates, being a different color, will either disagree, react, become silent, argue, or try to convince the other that his or her color is wrong. The mate might believe that his color, his personality, his way of seeing and doing things, is superior. And he tries to change, engulf, or blend the mate's color into his own, so that they are more similar in color. After all, each person tends to think that his or her color is superior.

This happens when people dishonor differences. They try to eliminate the differences that define them, and in doing so they emotionally suffocate their mates and stray from the path to intimacy.

When people learn to stop trying to change their mates' colors, and to simply honor the differences that make them unique, something amazing happens. When yellow and blue overlap just a bit, they make a green area. True intimacy is the green, or whatever color develops when two mates' unique and different colors are joined together. You're not losing, abandoning, or diluting your own color—your own identity—but coming together as two separate people with a new and beautiful blend of colors. You don't ever lose your color, but when you mix your color and your mate's color together, you start to get a little bit of green, and that's when you are finding the deeper levels of intimacy.

Discovering that my wife, Norma, has her own color—and that color represents her personal concerns, opinions, expectations, feelings, and needs, all of which can be radically different from mine—has gone a long way in helping me recognize, and honor, her differences. I learned to look at her, not as a threat to my individuality, but as an amazing person whose color, blended into mine, makes us stronger, better, more beautiful. She comes to me with her own culture, upbringing, parents, education, physical appearance, personality, habits—all of the infinite things that make her who she is. I honor her for her differences, her unique color, and that decision has taken our relationship to levels I couldn't have imagined when I was dead-set on changing her color to be closer to mine.

Back then, I believed that my color was superior; that my opinions, expectations, and concerns were greater than hers or better than hers or more important than hers. I never voiced it in those terms; I just made little comments about how I felt she was wrong about most things. Because she wasn't a really aggressive or forceful person—and I was—I really engulfed her, mixing my colors into hers. Not knowing how to recognize our differences, much less how to honor them, I stumbled along in the dance of conflict, stuck behind that infuriating wall.

Don't let this happen to you! Take a moment to take the following color test. Then, once you know your mate's unique colors, as well as your own, begin to honor those colors in your words, actions, and deeds.

How to determine your own unique color

and share the information with your mate.

Describe yourself, answering the following questions with a number
from 1 (least like me) through 10 (most like me).
The following questions will allow you to discover your unique "color":

RED/"Dominant Leader"

1. I like to be in charge whenever possible _____.
2. I'm very competitive _____.
3. Making decisions is easy for me _____.
4. I like to get things done in a hurry _____.
5. I am the first born in my family _____
6. It's hard for me to carry on a conversation with my mate if I don't know where we're heading in the conversation _____.
7. When I shop, I like to get in the store, buy what I came for and get out quickly _____.
8. When driving, I like to arrive at my destination in a hurry _____.
9. I can watch a ball game on TV even if I don't personally know the players _____.
10. I like to keep a certain safe distance with people so as not to be too controlled by them _____.
11. I feel the closest to my mate when we are doing some activity together _____.
12. I love to overcome challenging situations or obstacles _____.

Add up your score for questions 1–12 _____.

ORANGE/"People Person"

13. I'm usually very optimistic _____.
14. I'm fun loving _____.
15. I like variety _____.
16. I like to be around people all the time _____.
17. I am the baby of the family, last born _____.
18. I get energy from being with other people _____.
19. I think better with new ideas if I can say them out loud with others _____.
20. I don't mind telling others about personal happenings in my life _____.
21. It's hard for me to see negatives with new ideas, I usually think I can do it no matter what it is _____.
22. It's not that difficult for me to shoot a squirrel, if it's eating the food I set out for the birds _____.
23. I have a need to be included in most decisions that affect my life or marriage. I need mutual agreement and harmony in decision making _____.
24. I like to entertain and influence people _____.

Add up your score for questions 13–24 _____.

GREEN/"Loyal and Stable"

25. In the groups of people I associate with, I like all of us to cooperate as much as possible in our endeavors _____.
26. I tend to be very loyal to my friends so as not to hurt their feelings _____.
27. I like life to stay fairly constant, with not a lot of quick changes _____.
28. It's difficult for me to say no to a friend in need _____.
29. I'm a good listener _____.

30. When I shop, I like to touch various things on my way to picking out what I came for _____.
31. When driving, I like to be careful and courteous to the other drivers on my way to a destination _____.
32. I'm not really that interested in a sporting game unless I personally know some of the players _____.
33. I love to decorate and arrange my living areas to reflect who I am _____.
34. I feel the closest to my mate when we are sharing with each other in deep conversation _____.
35. I have a need to serve others _____ and/or receive genuine appreciation for my service _____.
36. I have a need to feel connected to my mate through talking _____.
37. I have a need to receive Tenderness, verbally _____ or physically _____.
38. If I had the money, I'd like giving gifts to others _____.

Add up your scores from 25–38 _____.

BLUE/"Detailed and Analytical"

39. I like to be as accurate as possible when discussing events with others _____.
40. I tend to be detailed in running my life and at work _____.
41. I like to get new ideas from others and then go by myself to think carefully about the ideas and consider every detail _____.
42. At the end of a busy day, I like to be alone for awhile to rejuvenate _____.
43. I like my personal life to be more private and not tell strangers everything about myself or family _____.
44. I tend to see the negatives when a new idea comes from others _____.
45. I tend to see what needs to be done to have a well-ordered house or office _____.
46. Generally, I have a need to live by the "rules" and have moderate order in my life _____.
47. I have a need to receive commitment from my mate to feel secure in love _____ and/or money _____.
48. I have a need to feel accepted by my mate for who I am _____ and/or for what I do _____.
49. I need to feel safe with my mate to be who I am _____.
50. I like to do things well so that what I do will last _____.
51. When given an assignment, I like to follow through _____.

Add up your scores from 39–51 _____.

Mark down your total scores for each color.

Red _____ Yellow _____ Green _____ Blue _____.

Because we're all a combination of colors—usually with one color dominating—you'll have scores in each of the color categories. The important thing is to recognize how you and your mate differ and then to remember—and honor—your unique differences/color combinations when conflict arise.

Now that you and your mate know your unique color combinations, begin honoring these colors in your actions, words, and deeds.

How to Honor Your Differences

In the last chapter, you learned that you and your mate have both acceptable differences and those that can cause discomfort. How you handle these differences can either bring you together or drive you apart.

Once you begin looking at differences as aspects to honor, instead of points of contention to debate, then you can begin to find the doorway in the wall of conflict. The practice of actually honoring these differences will allow you not only to see the doorway but also to walk through it into the new world of true intimacy.

You know what your differences are with your mate from the exercises in Chapter 4. Now, let's take action by honoring them.

Here's an example: "I really don't want to go to your mother's house this Christmas," a wife says to her husband. "We've gone there every year and it's always the same. She just puts me down all the time,"

The difference is obvious: she doesn't enjoy being with his mother as much as he does. What's the typical reply for the husband? The "dishonoring your differences" response. His first response will most likely be defensive. He feels vulnerable, protective of his mother, his family, his differences: "What's wrong with my mother?" he says. "Did you ever think that maybe you're the problem, not her? We're going and that's the end of this discussion."

This dishonoring response gets the dance of conflict going. The simple expression of an opinion—"We've gone there every year and it's always the same"—triggers an argument that will leave both parties emotionally bruised, reverting to more superficial levels of conversation or closing the door to communication altogether.

The "honoring your differences" response involves the husband's pausing to gather his thoughts, controlling his anger, remembering to honor above all, then trying to understand the difference that is being expressed through his wife's opinion. "I didn't know you felt that way," he might say. "Tell me how you feel so that I can understand your feelings."

Let me stress the most important part of this point: controlling your anger. Anger is the number one force that destroys honor and, just as a fire burns down a building, once anger begins, it can rage out of control. You must learn to keep your anger level low. When you feel anger, recognize it as a negative and subdue it as quickly as you can. How? By remembering how valuable you both are. Calm down, and repair your relationship by using all three skills: honor, drive-through listening (which we'll detail in Chapter 6), and recharging your mate's "needs battery" through love (which we'll discuss in Chapter 7). I've discovered that the best and easiest repair method for me is to simply stop and say, "I'm sorry. Will you forgive me?" At this juncture, your mate must also learn to forgive and move forward, realizing that valuable people screw up from time to time.

The difference between the honoring and dishonoring couples we've just detailed is easy to see. It's a difference of roles: as a daughter-in-law, she has one way of looking at his mother; as her son, he has another. It's a difference that will never change. When he honors that difference instead of making it an issue to argue, the discussion is elevated to a new level. The difference becomes a doorway; the couple can continue the discussion until they understand each other's feelings and needs. Then, and only then, in the safety of knowing that they will not be belittled, berated, or verbally abused, can they begin sharing their feelings and their needs, which are, of course, the two deepest levels of intimacy.

The chart below can better illustrate for you some of the differences you are likely to encounter and how your responses to them could honor or dishonor your mate:

Differences	Showing Dishonor	Showing Honor
Gender differences	"You sure are grumpy. Is it that time of the month?"	"Are you feeling all right? You seem to be pretty agitated. Is something bothering you?"
Opinions, concerns, expectations	"I don't care if you want to go away at Christmas; I am going to stay here and that's it!"	"Let's decide on a time to sit down and discuss what we want to do for the holidays, and we'll be able to make a compromise that will allow us both to enjoy the season."
Values	"I don't believe drinking alcohol is morally acceptable, and I don't want you to either."	"I do not drink alcohol for my own personal reasons, but I will not judge you if you want to have a drink in a social situation."
Personalities	"I want to go to the party and see my friends, and you have to come with me."	"It's important to me to see my friends at this party, but we can go in separate cars and if you are not enjoying yourself, I will understand if you want to leave earlier than I do."
Dreams	"It's stupid to dream about living on a boat. We'd never be able to afford it."	"Wow, wouldn't that be an adventure? I've never had that dream myself, but I am willing to think about it as a possibility."

When All Else Fails . . .

Here's an exercise to try the next time your mate states an opinion that reveals a difference between the two of you. How will you know it? It will be an opinion unique to his or her personality, and it will conflict with your own opinions or ideas. When it happens, don't be emotionally lazy; remember that the easiest response is the quickest. Resist the temptation for knee-jerk, angry reactions when your mate voices a basic difference in philosophy, emotions, or needs. Even if you aren't exactly certain of the most productive response, try this: be a good LUVR (pronounced LO·ver), an anagram that means:

> **Listen** to your mate's feelings.
> **Understand** them.
> **Validate** his or her unique perspective without judgment.
> **Respect and respond** to his or her perspectives and honor them as his or her own, not yours, and by making an effort to find a solution that will attend to both your needs and feelings. In this way, you actually blend your two colors.

If you make sure you are being a good LUVR in every situation, you will ensure that you are making your relationship a safe environment for your mate to share his or her feelings and needs with you, even if you don't immediately have the best or most appropriate response at your fingertips.

Honoring your differences serves two purposes. First, you are validating your mate, making him or her feel secure to show you feelings and needs. Second, you are imbuing yourself and your mate with the power to move in the direction of intimate communication, which leads toward the two deepest levels. By making this commitment—"I admit that we have many differences, but these differences will no longer be a point of contention, but instead a place for greater understanding"— you are creating a foundation for intimacy. You're not giving up your own opinions or adjusting your differences to become identical with your mate. You are merely allowing yourself to see your mate's viewpoint in a new, tolerant light and thus opening the door to intimacy. Once you make this decision, your relationship will immediately move to a deeper level. Your mate will feel secure enough to tell you his or her feelings and needs, and you will feel safe enough to share yours. You will begin meeting one of the most pivotal needs inherent to every human being: the need to be valued.

It's going to take practice. After all, we're talking about changing years, perhaps decades, of conditioned responses. We're talking about transforming typical negative responses into positive ones. Human beings aren't robots; you can't turn a key and make every negative response come out positive. But you can condition yourself, gradually, to control your negative reactions—an important first step toward honoring. You can learn to look for the positive side of things before allowing your aggravation to lure you down the path of dishonor.

The Second Act of Honor: The Honor List

In my seminars, I compare the cumulative results of consistent honoring to building a strong, rock-solid lighthouse. The practice of consistent honoring is like a construction project—in this case, the building of a lighthouse. Once you break ground, you will begin to see immediate improvements in your relationship. The stones of the lighthouse are every "honoring" word you speak, write, or convey through your actions to your mate; these granite stones will lift your lighthouse higher and safer from the storms. The light in the lighthouse will be your personal inventory of all the things you cherish and value about your mate. The more complete your inventory, the brighter your light will be.

Once you have built your lighthouse with strong, high foundations, your relationship will be a safer vessel to steer. No matter what storms you may encounter, if your honor is set in the stone of the lighthouse, the bright light will almost always guide you back to the safe harbor of love and intimacy.

Here's how to begin to build your own lighthouse of honor:

1. List all the things you cherish about your mate. The longer the list, the stronger your honor, the brighter the light of that lighthouse. When you're facing conflict, return to your list. It will give you strength and inspire honor, because how can you dishonor when you're staring at such a long list of specific honorable traits? Post this list in a highly visible place in your home where you and, more important, your mate can see it every day. Everyone has great qualities about them. Consider the traits of your mate's personality (introverted vs. extroverted), appearance, thinking patterns, gender differences, faith patterns, shared values, parenting skills, concerns, opinions, and life goals. Personalize your list! Let your mate see your list then exchange lists regularly.

2. List the things you are grateful for your mate providing in your life. What do you have today that you wouldn't have without your mate? A truly happy person is a grateful person. Look around and see what you have now. Personally, what has been a really great benefit to me in this area is my faith in God. I am constantly aware of what God provides for me through creation and answers to prayer. I'm more able to reach out and value my mate because I am so filled as a person myself. If we concentrate on what we have instead of what we don't have, our attitude is so much more alive and it's so much easier to honor others.

3. List all the ordinary things that you love about your mate. Life is not all picnics and pansies. Life is more frequently a succession of ordinary occurrences, but these, too, you must learn to honor. So list the ordinary occurrences: the way he or she handles daily work, washes the car, cleans the garage, brushes his or her hair, takes out the garbage. Find the bright light in the ordinarily dark corners. Once you begin to see your mate totally—including the ordinary—then you can honor the person completely.

4. List all the things you dislike about your mate and learn to "treasure hunt," an important tool to employ in building a rock-solid, towering lighthouse of honor. Remember, you and your mate have committed yourselves to consider each other as not only very valuable but the most valuable things on

earth, worthy of reverence, praise, and honor without restriction. You have committed yourself to treating each other as *treasures*, and that attitude governs all your actions and words, even when potentially negative situations arise. So when negative situations, words, and actions come along—and they certainly will—learn to search for the positive, the treasure, to focus upon. Treasure hunting involves the conscious seeking of the positives within the negatives. I have always been able to find some positive aspect of any negative occurrence. To treasure-hunt, you must ask yourself: "What can I learn or have learned from my mate's potentially dislikable traits? What would I have to do to turn the negative perception into a positive?"

Discovering the treasures beneath your trials is the fastest way I know to raise your self-worth and your perception of your relationships. The following exercise is one my wife and I use to discover the treasures in our personal trials. Perhaps it will work for you as well.

Divide a piece of paper into six columns and label the columns as follows: (1) What I like about myself; (2) What I like about my mate; (3) Our past trials; (4) Support and helpful skills; (5) Benefits from trials; (6) Love in action.

What I like about myself	What I like about my mate	Our past trials	Support and helpful skills	Benefits from trials	Love in action

In the first two columns, list at least three things you like about yourself and three things you like about your mate.

In the third column, list the issues that have caused you and your mate arguments, stress, and tension. These are the painful experiences that cause anger, bitterness, and varying levels of grief. Some people have told me it's too painful to list all of these trials at one time, so you may prefer to focus on one or two for the moment and deal with others at another time.

In the fourth column, list the people who have helped you through your more serious trials and/or the skills you or your mate used to work through things and resolve your problems successfully. Maybe you have found word pictures to be helpful, or maybe your church pastor has helped counsel you and your mate through some rough spots.

In the fifth column, list whatever benefits you can think of that came as a result of your trial. If you can't think of any at first, try to remember that trials can produce various aspects of love—try to think if the trial helped you love yourself or your mate more.

In the final column, list ways in which the benefits of the trial have changed your behavior. The purpose of trials is to help us know and love ourselves and our mates better.

You may still doubt that your own trials have any buried treasure, so let's look at some examples.

Decide to consider your mate's ideas, thinking, opinions, concerns, expectations, and life goals as just a little more important than your own. This is the best way to increase honor. This attitude will bring more life and positive experiences into your marriage than anything else. But it's the hardest step and easiest to forget. Your mate will see the change instantly—and you will begin to increase the honor and esteem in which you hold your mate.

Learn to communicate, especially through drive-through listening—the most powerful communications method on earth, which we'll explain fully in the next chapter—when you have a serious disagreement. When you are a LUVR, it builds honor into the relationship and the person you honor feels more valued.

When you discover the main needs of your mate and dedicate yourself to spending a few minutes a day to help meet those needs, your mate sees your new commitment to his or her value. Honor increases with each attempt to creatively meet the needs of your mate.

Commit yourself to building a lighthouse of honor in your relationship. Once you do that, you'll protect yourself from the storms that will come. The higher the honor, the safer your relationship will be from harm. Once you build your lighthouse, you will begin to come closer to your mate in a very real and profound way. When you make honor a priority, and begin posting and proclaiming your honor on a daily basis, you'll be ready for reaching the destination on the ultimate relationship roadmap, the place where your mate keeps all of his or her feelings and needs, the most profound place on earth—the house of the heart.

As you begin practicing honor on a daily basis, you'll want to try as many of the following modes of honor as possible in your contact with your mate.

1. *Communication methods.* Genuine communication, through proven techniques such as word pictures or drive-through listening, is the fastest route to your mate's heart. It's the most direct way to tell your partner that you really want to hear of his or her feelings and needs; that you want to make your discussions as meaningful and comfortable as possible; that you honor your partner's feelings and needs and will genuinely listen to him or her. In the book *Lasting Marriages,* longtime happily married couples commented on the skills that helped them sustain their marriages. Guess what was on the top of the list? "We talk, talk, talk," one wife, who had been happily married for more than fifty years, told a researcher. "We've never done anything without talking about it. We don't let anything burn inside us. We don't agree on everything, but I respect him for the way he thinks, and he respects me."

2. *Dealing with anger.* Anger is the enemy of honor. The moment you lash out at your mate, honor flies out the window. Think about it: when you respond through your temper, in words, actions, or attitudes, you are basically shutting the door to honor. How you control your anger shows your level of

honor for your mate. Does your mate deserve to be yelled at, to be called names, to be accused? No. Honoring your mate means showing that person that you consider him or her worthy of praise and, when necessary, your forgiveness. Make one hard-and-fast rule: when the disagreement is done, no matter the outcome, you will forgive your mate. Said one wife in *Lasting Marriages*, "Remember the golden rule. You don't snap their heads off, you don't throw things, you don't scream and cry. Be patient. Be willing to bend."

3. *Meeting physical needs.* Physical contact is honor in action. Studies show that women need to be touched—a hug, a kiss, a warm embrace—at least eight times a day to maintain balance in their bodies. Human beings have an inherent need to be touched; newborn babies can actually die from the lack of physical contact. Whether it is a simple caress on the cheek, a held hand, a stroke on the hair, your touch speaks volumes— it's the physical translation of love and honor. As the passions of young love subside and mature love sets in, it is natural for the physical aspects of a relationship to wane. Don't let it happen! Become determined to maintain physical contact, even if it's only small gestures. A ritual kiss on your way out the door in the morning is better than no kiss at all. Remember, physical contact is the cellular maintenance for honor and love. Don't allow it to perish in your relationship!

4. *Nurturing.* The Greek word for nurturer is *husbandman,* which in farming terms means a professional gardener, someone who tills the soil and tends to the plants. A nurturer helps things grow. In the garden, that means watering the plants and keeping them out in the sun. In the field of relationships, nurturing means much the same thing. Nurturing is an essential aspect of honor because it involves tending to your partner's feelings and needs. Think of it in terms of gardening. How do you make your plants grow? Certainly not by yelling at them. You make plants grow through your attention. The same is true for intimacy. Nurturing has four different parts, four nonnegotiable ingredients: deep-seated security, meaningful conversation, emotional or romantic times, and positive physical touching.

5. *Using trials to grow.* This goes back to your attitude about conflict. It honors your mate when you see conflict as an opportunity for growth and intimacy instead of as a failure in your relationship. Try to maintain the attitude that you are in this relationship for life, and that you never stop learning from the little bumps in the road. It honors your mate when you take the attitude that conflict is a small thing compared to the larger importance of your love and bond. As one wife said in the book *Lasting Marriages*, "Sure you're gonna have some conflicts, you're gonna have some arguments. It's silly to think you're not. What kind of relationship would that be? But they're not serious enough to create any real problem."

6. *Making unhealthy relationships healthy.* If you find yourself caught in a dishonoring relationship, you're going to have to do some soul-searching with each other. Begin by asking your mate these three questions: (1) On a scale of from 1 to 10, with 1 being terrible and 10 being great, where would you like our relationship to be? (2) On a scale of from 1 to 10, overall, where would you rate our relationship today? (3) As you look at our relationship, what are some specific things we could do over the next six weeks that would move us closer to a 10? Once you get your mate's answers, do not forget, deny, or dismiss them. Keep asking him or her to help you understand what she is saying and keep at it until it makes sense!

7. *Setting personal boundaries.* Yes, we all want intimacy, but everyone also needs boundaries. The mission of intimacy requires discovering your mate's personal boundaries and honoring them. It is honoring when you give a person the space and time alone.

Recognizing Dishonor

The opposite of honor—dishonor—is the most destructive force you can inflict upon your relationship. When we dishonor others, we consciously or unknowingly treat them as if they have little value, usually through unjust criticism, unhealthy comparisons, favoritism, inconsistency, jealousy, selfishness, envy, and a host of other verbal and mental artillery.

Dishonor can be subtle, but I have learned to look for a mental "red alarm." Anytime you feel that you are superior to your mate, that your thinking is more valid, your concerns are more important, your talents are better, your expectations are more accurate, you instantly send yourself straight back to the cold side of the wall of conflict and to more superficial levels of intimacy. Even worse, feelings of superiority could eventually send you straight to divorce court.

Here's a story illustrating how natural it is to think that your ideas are somehow better than your mate's. A couple of years ago, my wife and I had a disagreement over how to complete our will for our children. We couldn't agree and it was always painful to discuss it. I suggested that we meet with three friends who might help us think through this potentially explosive issue in a calm and honoring way. On the way to our friends' house, I opened my big trap and suggested that Norma would feel embarrassed when she soon heard from our "advisors" how her reasoning was seriously flawed. I was dead-set on believing that my ideas were better than hers. Well, you can imagine how she reacted! But when our friends heard us out, they all agreed, including me, that Norma's ideas were better. Norma was a little nervous at this outcome because she thought that I would be upset. I wasn't, however, and the instance showed me how natural it is to think our opinions are somewhat superior.

In my book *Love is a Decision*, I outlined the top ten most dishonoring acts in any home, as reported by couples I'd interviewed. See if any of these are familiar to you:

1. Ignoring or degrading another person's opinions, advice, or beliefs (especially criticizing another person's faith).
2. Burying oneself in front of the television or in the newspaper when another person is trying to communicate.
3. Creating jokes about another person's weak areas or

shortcomings (sarcasm or cutting jokes act like powerful emotional word pictures and do lasting harm in a relationship).

4. Making regular verbal attacks on loved ones: criticizing harshly, being judgmental, delivering uncaring lectures.

5. Treating in-laws or other relatives as unimportant in one's planning and communication.

6. Ignoring or simply not expressing appreciation for kind deeds done for us.

7. Distasteful habits that are practiced in front of the family, even after we are asked to stop.

8. Overcommitting ourselves to other projects or people, so that everything outside the home seems more important than those inside the home.

9. Power struggles that leave one person feeling that he or she is a child or is being harshly dominated.

10. An unwillingness to admit that we are wrong or ask for forgiveness.

Do any of these sound familiar? If so, you probably have a problem with dishonor in your home or relationship. But all is not lost; if there is even a spark of honor in you and your mate's hearts, we can fan it into a flame.

Here's another exercise to help you treasure-hunt:

How to Find the Positive Side to Your Mate's Negative Traits

In my previous books, I've compared turning negative responses into positives to treasure hunting—taking what was said or done that was discouraging or disheartening in the past and turning it into something positive, something from which you can learn and grow. Here's a chart to get you started. Insert your mate's negative traits and reframe them into positive perceptions. Once you get the concept, begin practicing turning "negative" aspects into positive perceptions. It's the essence of honor.

Negative Trait	Positive Perception
Nosy	He or she may be overly alert or sociable
Touchy	He or she may be very sensitive
Manipulating	He or she may be a very resourceful person with many creative ideas
Stingy	He or she may be very thrifty
Talkative	He or she may be very expressive or dynamic
Flighty	He or she may be an enthusiastic person with cheerful vitality
Too serious	He or she may be very sincere and earnest with strong convictions
Too bold	He or she may have strong convictions, uncompromising with his or her own standards
Rigid	He or she may be a well-disciplined person with strong convictions
Overbearing	He or she may be a very confident person—sure of him or herself
A dreamer	He or she may be very creative and imaginative
Too fussy	He or she may be very organized and efficient

How Honor Can Transform Arguments into Healthy Conversations

It's easy to have an argument: all you have to do is follow your natural emotions and impulses, wherever they lead, even if it's out the slamming door in a storm of raining clothes and flatware. It's harder to have a conversation, which involves logic, attention, and frequently restraint. Yes, conversations take more work, but they are infinitely more rewarding; arguments take you apart, while conversations bring you together.

No relationship is without its disagreements. But if you employ the principles of honor to your disagreements, you can transform a potential argument into an educational, even an enlightening conversation. Let me show you how radically different a disagreement can become once a couple feels safe enough to share feelings and needs without fear of being dishonored.

"I'm afraid we're going to fight about money," said a man to his fiancée. It was a simple opinion, but opinions can be dangerous, and this one struck Susan like a bullet. She and her fiancé, George, had a fairy-tale romance—they rarely fought because they respected each other and enjoyed spending time together. She was excited to spend the rest of her life with him and to raise children with him. They both knew they had differences, but up until now those differences had posed no threat to their relationship. "What do you mean, exactly?" she asked hesitantly.

"I'm just worried," George said with a sigh. "I think we have really different opinions about money and how to use it."

He had taken the first step toward honor: admitting differences in an open, nonthreatening way. But even with this gentle approach, Susan felt threatened. She knew that the differences existed between her and her future husband, but to her it had been no big deal. She had been raised by parents who believed in "living in the moment": they saved, but they never made themselves want for anything. She had grown up with an unlimited supply of spending money. She never worried about saving, and she was secure in knowing that her parents would help her financially for as long as she needed it. Since graduation from college, Susan had been trying to make a career in the entertainment industry, and until now she had been forced to take low-paying but rewarding jobs that she saw as investments in her future. As a result, she had no chance to save any money yet and was still semidependent on her parents. But she saw herself as generally responsible about money, and she knew the value of a dollar.

George, on the other hand, was, well, different. He had been raised by a single mother who had grown up in post-World War II Europe. Although his family was wealthy now, they had not always been so, and from childhood he had been taught to save wherever possible. Therefore, even though he was in graduate school, he had saved money from inheritances and was proud of his ability to save. He wanted to hang onto his savings until he could retire early and spend quality time with his future family. "Well, I don't see any big problem, but let's discuss your feelings," replied Susan, honoring the difference instead of becoming embattled. "What do you think will make us fight?"

"I am just worried," said George. "You're always going to the mall, buying clothes and other stuff. You haven't saved any money, and I don't want to feel like my savings will be threatened. I need to know that you can be smart about money."

Now, Susan forgot about honoring differences and became angry and defensive. "Of course I can be smart!" she shouted, throwing honor out the window. "How dare you criticize me? I've worked so hard, but in my career, you can't make a lot of money in the beginning; you have to pay your dues! I haven't had a chance to save any money!"

George knew he had triggered an emotional defense from Susan, yet he didn't match her shouts with his own. Amid the heat of disagreement, he spoke from a position of honor. First, he validated her: "I know you're responsible and smart, Susan, and I love you," he began. Then, he put his words in an honor-bound framework: "I'm just telling you my feelings. You complain about not having money but you spend it anyway, and that worries me."

"George, most times I go to the mall I don't end up buying a thing," Susan replied, in a conversational tone, now that she felt safe to share. "It's a way of winding down for me from the high stress level of my job. And when I do buy things, I spend my money wisely. I'm not just throwing money away. I expect you to give me that benefit of the doubt."

"I guess I just never thought about it that way," said George. "You have to understand, I just hear you complain about it, then you come home with a shopping bag, and I don't understand why."

"George, we spend money in different ways, but that doesn't make either one of us 'irresponsible' compared to the other. You don't like to go shopping, but you love expensive vacations," Susan pointed out. "I never go on exotic vacations; I like just visiting family and friends.' "

"That's true," George replied. "I just need to know that when we get married, you will respect my money and your money and *our* money and you will think about all our needs every day. I need to know that I will not be the only one having to say, 'Wait, hold on, let's think about this,' " George said.

Notice he's already sharing feelings and needs. By honoring their differences and discussing them, he's taking himself and his mate through the doorway toward intimacy.

"That's fair enough," agreed Susan. "But what I need from you is respect—you must respect that the choices I make are informed and thought out, that I am a responsible adult, and if you have concerns, you should discuss them *with* me, not tell me what to do."

This potentially explosive disagreement led to greater understanding by both parties. Before, Susan had generally considered George stingy, while George had considered Susan a bit of a spendthrift. But when both talked about how they each felt about their financial situations, they realized that both of them were guilty of dishonoring the other. Instead of respecting their choices and their feelings, they had silently degraded each other's opinions because they were different from their own. Now, at least they knew the reasons behind the differences.

The conversation had started as a tense one—and the first in which either Susan or George had ever expressed doubts about their impending life together—but Susan actually felt relieved after they talked. "He felt comfortable talking to me about his feelings, even though they weren't exactly pleasant," she says. "And throughout the entire conversation, even when things got tense, he always showed that he was making an effort to hear my thoughts and feelings, to keep his mind flexible. That showed me how much he does care about me, that although he was concerned, he was at least trying not to judge me. I feel like I know him a little bit better now, and I feel more at ease knowing he knows that much more about me."

Through honoring each other, they had defused an argument that would have surely caused them problems later in their marriage. Susan and George used their point of contention as a place for greater understanding.

Try to do the same the next time you find yourself in an argument. We've talked about how to defuse conflicts in the earlier chapters, and using honor only makes the process more simple:

1. *Control your anger.* This is the biggie, the nuclear bomb of relationships. You must learn to see anger as the fuse on a very real bomb during disagreements. Remember: disagreements are only the expression of differences. Discover the differences that are behind the argument, instead of falling prey to your first emotion, anger. Stopping conflict from escalating through anger is the most effective way to ensure that it will not become destructive. Here's a simple, yet effect way: *count to 10.* It's that simple! Just count to 10 before responding to a potential disagreement. Honor first, then act. It will derail your anger and allow you to dive to the deeper levels.

2. *Constantly remember, and reinforce, your honor.* Deciding to honor is the first move you must make, but remembering and reinforcing the decision during heated conversations with your mate is absolutely essential. Your first reaction will be to get angry and focus on blaming or venting your frustrations. But you must learn to consciously and continually give your mate priority over those emotions. Honoring means giving your mate distinction above fleeting emotions and giving his or her feelings validation without judgment.

3. *Ask for help.* If you don't understand your mate's perspective, ask him or her to help you. Again, it's just that simple—and just that powerful. Ask for clarification, for word pictures, for directions, to help you see things from your mate's point of view. Begin by assuming that his or her perspective is valid, and then seek to understand it. Believe me, your mate will feel honored that you asked.

Always look for the "win-win" solution because, believe it or not, the win-win situation always exists. Honor goes both ways. Both you and your mate must establish a bedrock of honor to be successful in your quest for an intimate and successful relationship. One-sided honor never works! Therefore, you must assume that in any disagreement, both of your feelings are valid. Look for solutions that not only compromise but also collaborate—so that neither of you sacrifices your own opinions, feelings, and needs. Combine your opinions, don't eliminate them. It is hoped you will be able to find answers that will make both of you happy.

Take a moment to check off your mate's positive characteristics, qualities, and attributes from the following list, to which you can add your own qualities.

___ Kind	___ Successful
___ Smart	___ Creative
___ Attractive	___ Talented
___ Giving	___ Resourceful
___ Funny	___ Friendly
___ Spirited	___ Considerate

The Third Act of Honor: Proclaim It!

Once you've decided to honor your differences and have made a complete listing, an inventory, of everything to honor, it's time for the third act of the honor process.

Say it, write it, post it!

Proclaim it!

Honor cannot exist in silence. Just consider a crowd at a football game, or the audience of a hit movie, or the congregation at a wedding. They don't honor in silence the victorious team, the movie stars, or the blushing couple. No, that honor explodes in cheering, applause, and tears. This is the type of honor you have to inject into your relationship. Proclaiming honor has power, once you make it known, you lift up and expose it so everyone can see it.

It can be as easy as posting a photograph or buying a gift, for no reason except to say, "I honor you."

Shortly after Norma startled me out of my relational malaise with the statement I detailed earlier in this chapter— "Gary, I feel that everything on earth is more important to you than I am!"—I made a vow to honor her above all worldly things in my words, actions, and deeds. To begin, I created a hall of honor in a prominent place in our home. Its walls are filled with pictures and letters, but the plaque that means the most to me proclaims, "To Norma, Kari, Greg, and Michael, Presented to My Family for Assurance of My Lifetime Commitment . . . Gary T. Smalley." The plaque and the paraphernalia that surround it is tangible proof of my undying devotion and commitment, and it's the essence of honor, so necessary to the growth of any relationship.

Hardly one week goes by that I don't remind my wife that I honor her. But words are not the only ingredients in honor. Words are the currency of all too many people who said one thing and then act in another way, leaving their mates with a hall of shame instead of a hall of honor. So to establish real honor in your relationship, to create a true bedrock on which intimacy can be built, you have to not merely proclaim and post your commitment but also learn how to act on it every day. Every time you act in an honoring way you're adding to your hall of honor in your home, until your house—and your relationship—becomes a testament to the victory of intimacy.

It's now time to reestablish a sense of ceremony and courtship in your relationship. Begin by posting a photograph from your courtship in a prominent place in your home. This is a simple act, yet a profound way of showing honor to your mate, merely by showing that you honor your memories together. The photograph has extraordinary power; it is evidence—tangible proof—of all that your relationship once was and what it can once again become. It will show your mate that you cherish, and thus honor, him or her.

Here are two useful exercises to help you honor your mate:

Write Letters to Your Mate

Do you remember when you first fell in love with your mate? That rush, that urgency that made you breathless when you were near him or her? Couples first in love are often overcome by the well of emotions that accompanies it, and they are the most likely to write love letters.

It does wonders to receive a letter of love, but it does even more to write one. Set aside a half hour and sit down with pen and paper—your own handwriting will mean even more to you both—and write a love letter to your mate. It doesn't have to be long, it doesn't have to be overly sentimental, just express your feelings, tell how you feel, list the little things that you admire and appreciate about him or her. Then leave the letter, sealed, where your mate will find it on the kitchen counter, propped on a pillow, taped to the bathroom mirror. You will be amazed at how much you and your mate will be energized by the expression of love and honor.

Keep an "Honor Book"

It is a common practice to keep scrapbooks and photograph albums of family events. But what about keeping a scrapbook exclusively for you and your mate? It can work magic in the honor department. "An Honor Book" chronicles your romance, your history together helps you remember to honor both your mate and your relationship.

Here's how to create one:

1. Obtain either a medium-sized box (with a secure lid) or a scrapbook album.
2. Fill the album's pages with memories of only you and your mate—you can keep other albums for your family, but this is just for the two of you. Include photographs, souvenirs (such as matchbooks, cards, ticket stubs), quotes from movies or songs, inside jokes or sayings that the two of you understand. One person I know even saved the spoons she and her mate used to eat ice cream on a date in college. At the time, they were just like any plastic spoons they used any day. Now,

she looks at them and remembers exactly how it felt to walk along the campus sidewalk by her now-husband's side, how excited she was to be out on a date with him.

3. You don't necessarily have to keep the album in chronological order, but everything you put into the Honor Book should be labeled so that you will be able to identify it and remember its significance.

4. Keep your Honor Book in a safe but accessible spot, where either you or your mate can easily reach it, and keep scissors, a permanent marker, and glue or tape with it so that you never have to work too hard to add to the book. Bring the book out on occasions like Valentine's Day, your anniversary, or even Christmas.

5. Share your book with your children. It is important to show them the love and honor between their parents. Somewhere you should include either a written or audiotaped version of the story of how you met your mate, preferably with both of you contributing. Someday, this will become a treasure to them, as it was to you: a permanent remnant of your voice, either written or verbal, telling the story of your love.

Once you begin practicing honor, a powerful alchemy will occur in your relationship: your honoring words, actions, and deeds will propel you through the wall of conflict into the promised land of intimacy. Once you're there, you'll be ready to stay by learning and practicing the most powerful communication method on earth, a method of turning conversations, even heated conversations, into a means for descending deeper into greater honor and deeper intimacy, instead of an exit door through which to flee back to the shallowest levels of half-hearted love.

CHAPTER SIX

Drive-Through Listening: The Greatest Communication Method on Earth

Skill Number 2
Drive Thru Listening

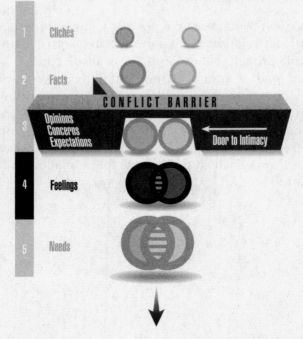

COMMUNICATION IS, OF COURSE, PARAMOUNT in relationships, the primary way we share our feelings and needs, the key to entering the deepest levels of intimacy, the medium through which we show our mates who we are. The other four human senses—touch, feel, smell, taste—are mighty, but in relationships the fifth sense of hearing reigns supreme. But optimum communication begins with *listening*, not with searching for solutions. Listening is the basis of honor. Every human being needs to be heard, just as surely as they need to be fed.

Being human, when we hear something even remotely problematic or potentially threatening—especially something threatening from our mate—the natural reaction is to avoid it or to try and search for a solution. So instead of paying full attention to what our mate is saying, we try to fix the perceived problem. Then, if we hit the wall of conflict, we run back to the shallowest levels of intimacy. And the majestic powers of communication, speaking and listening, the true art forms of love, become wasted in the halfway conversation of clichés and facts.

Whether you experience true intimacy or exile yourself to the superficial levels depends on the quality of your communication with your mate. There is a glut of material on communication, as any glance along bookstore shelves or at Internet Web pages will show. In my research, I've drawn from a variety of sources, including Harvel Hendricks's book *Getting the Love You Want*, his Imago organization, and his A Couples Workshop; Drs. Howard Markman, Scott Stanley, and Susan Blumberg's excellent program PREP; Sherod Miller's book *Couples Communication;* Dr. John Gottman's workshop; Dr. David Olson's training; and a host of others. But in my thirty years of study, the best explanation of optimum communication—and the best technology to make optimum communication occur—comes from a husband-and-wife relationship team in Arizona, Dr. Dallas and Nancy Demmitt. They call their technique Bridging.

"To put it simply, most of the struggles we experience—whether in relationship with God, spouse, or a colleague—center on a breakdown in communication," they write in their *Bridging Workshop* workbook. "Fix the communication and the relationship can heal. Unfortunately, many people have a wrong concept about what communication is about. Most people treat the process of communication like an airplane ride. They have a place they want to take us—and they want to get us there as quickly as possible. Others see communication as a subway—with a pre-planned route, unmovable guidelines, and a 'hidden' agenda beneath the surface. But in reality, good communication is more like a bridge—where two people can work diligently to span the seemingly uncrossable gulf in their relationship—coming together from opposite directions to understand, pool resources, and unite around common goals. The bridge is built so each person can get to the other side: the deepest levels of intimacy with their mate. Here, they can see the world from a different perspective—their mate's. They can travel freely back and forth, widening their viewpoint and enriching their experiences. The goal of communication is to gain understanding, to discover hidden resources, and to pool resources for mutually satisfying results."

I love the Demmitts' analogy: two mates separated by a gulf of differences, each most likely desiring the same destination—intimacy—but enshrouded by clouds about how to get there. Often, you can't see the bridge because you're buffeted by the storms of conflict with its accompanying gales of confusion. Once the storm clears, you can see the bridge. It's not a literal bridge, but an ideological one: optimal communication involves communicating in conflict. Too many of us suffer the stereotypical conditioning that "communicating in conflict" means arguing—something to run from instead of embrace as a learning experience—so some seldom cross the bridge into our mate's domain. We remain on our own side, stuck in our own preconceptions, beliefs, values, and ideas, and thus we might not cross the line to real intimacy often enough.

Are you ready to *honor* your mate with the most valuable gift you can give him or her at this moment—your complete, undivided attention?

Learn to Drive-Through Listen

In this chapter, I'm going to show you how to cross that bridge, and to enter the depths of intimacy whenever necessary, by employing the most powerful communications method on earth, a conversational technique that, once mastered, will help you remain in the deepest level of intimacy. It's not going to cost you a nickel except for your time. But it can result in nothing short of a revolution in your relationship. So let down your guard and open your mind to the secrets of optimum communication—and prepare yourself to discover more of the brave new world of your mate's heart: drive-through listening.

Drive-through listening can save your marriage, enrich it, and play a major part in moving you into and helping you remain in the fourth and fifth levels of intimacy. It automatically eliminates the four main causes of divorce. Don't be tempted to see this method as some complicated, advanced computer science. If my friends and I can learn it, as well as thousands of my seminar participants, I know that you can, too. It's so easy that virtually everyone, from children to the elderly, all over the world are already using it. It's a method practiced by fast-food employees, some of them teenagers not even out of high school. You've certainly already used the method, too, every time you wanted a hamburger, taco, or chicken or roast beef sandwich. So if you can order a hamburger, you can master the most effective way to optimum relationship conversation.

Here is the essence of drive-through listening:

Imagine you are driving up to a fast-food restaurant, and you pull into the drive-through lane. You stop at the speaker, study the menu, and decide what you want to order for you and your family. The clerk's voice booms from the intercom: "Hello, welcome to The Happy Meal. May I take your order, please?"

"Yes, I would like two hamburgers, two cheeseburgers, two Cokes, one Diet Coke, three orders of large fries, and one order of chicken tenders, please," you'll reply. To make sure everything's correct, you'll turn and ask your family, "All right?"

"Right!" they agree.

The voice in the speaker booms back, "Okay. That'll be three hamburgers, one cheeseburger, two Diet Cokes, one Coke, three fries, and a chicken tender."

"Uh, no, wait," you'll respond quickly. "I said two hamburgers, two cheeseburgers, two Cokes, one Diet Coke, and the three fries and the one chicken tender pack."

"Oh, I'm sorry, sir. Let me try again. Two hamburgers, two cheeseburgers, two Cokes, one Diet Coke, three fries, and a chicken tender?"

You're relieved that they've gotten your order loud and clear. "That's right, that's it," you'll reply.

"Great. That'll be $13.85. Please pull around to the first window, sir," the voice booms.

Notice that the attendant doesn't get off track. He doesn't say, "Okay, sir, but are you aware of the fat grams in the large french fries?" Or, "I can see you're a little overweight; why not try the low-cal chicken sandwich?" Or, even worse, "Sir, I can't stand cheeseburgers. Could you please order something I enjoy serving?" No, he maintains focus strictly on your order; otherwise, he'd probably be fired. He's not trained to give opinions about your needs. We all know why it would be bad business for a fast-food franchise employee to respond to a customer with personal interpretations about an order. The customer would probably "divorce" the company eventually, especially if the clerk's opinion turns out to be wrong.

But the same type of "divorce" can strike our homes. Without simple training, we bombard our mates will all types of extraneous opinions when they're trying to tell us what they feel, need, or want. At the fast-food franchise, you simply place your order, they repeat it back to you, and when you get to the window, they hand you your sack. You get everything you ordered, thanks to the careful verbal repetition and confirmation of your desires and needs to the ever-friendly fast-food clerk. You avoid the frustration of driving away and discovering you have a bag full of chicken tenders when you wanted a hamburger.

Yes, it's frustrating to be misunderstood. That is why fast-food franchises, specializing in fast, efficient service, employ the method of drive-through communication. You state your desires to someone—in other words, you "place your order." The sales clerk strives to ensure that he or she has heard your order correctly so that she meets your feelings and needs precisely. Therefore, she repeats what you said, clearly and concisely, so that you can confirm it. If she repeats your order correctly, you can tell her, "Yes, that is what I mean, you understand me." If she does not repeat your order accurately, you can tell her, "No, that is not what I want. Let me repeat it for you or say it in another way to help you understand." You can keep doing this until the person does understand you, and then you know that you have clearly communicated.

It's a sad situation that we live in a world where our burger orders are communicated better than our personal feelings and needs. But most of us have never learned the strategies of ultimate relationship conversation. When it comes to getting what we need and want from the most important person in our lives—our mates—we stammer and mumble, rush in or storm out, reaping only frustration.

There is, however, a better way.

Three Key Thoughts to Keep in Mind . . .

1. You are learning to use drive-through listening in order to enter the deepest levels of intimacy and return there regularly.
2. Your mission is to enrich your marriage, and this method is the proven way.
3. You want to avoid the four main risk factors for divorce, and you can do that by using this method of communication.

If I Had Known Then What I Know Now . . .

If only Norma and I had known how to use drive-through listening early in our marriage, we could have avoided years of firing painful verbal salvos at each other from our respective banks across a river of differences, instead of simply walking across the bridge between our hearts. Couples seeking ultimate relationships must decide on their roles in every conversation. This is the key to every successful relationship: In the drive-through analogy, one of you must be the customer (the speaker), the other the clerk (the listener). You cannot both be customers, each of you trying to win your own points of view. This only leads to conflict, anger, argument, and falling into the four divorce patterns. If you truly want to create a long-lasting, loving, intimate relationship, you must choose your roles in every conversation. This is especially true if the conversation becomes heated with separate opinions, concerns, or expectations.

How do you decide who gets which role? I suggest employing the element of honor, always striving to let your mate take the customer (speaker) role as much as possible. This way, you let him or her do the talking, the "ordering," while you do the listening. Always strive to be the person who listens first, seeks to understand the other person first, and lets the other know that you value what he or she is saying because it reflects the honor you hold for who that person is. Realize that any angry, destructive argument can be transformed into a loving conversation immediately—if you will revert to the clerk role. Remember the saying, "The customer is always right"? That's because successful companies realize that they must listen carefully to their clients and strive to understand them and value their desires. Every successful salesman I've ever met is able to create successful solutions to a customer's concerns through careful listening and understanding. It's the same in relationships.

Consider this story. One day, my wife and I were planning to leave for a camping trip, which we had discovered as a way to spend quality time together. I got up early to jog, and while I was running I had what I thought was a great idea—I wanted to do something special and unexpected for Norma, just to show her some love and honor. I knew that she liked to have breakfast with her friend Helen, so I decided I'd encourage her to have breakfast out with her friend while I packed the camper. That way, when she got home she could simply slide into the front seat and—voila!—we would embark upon our journey into the wilderness. I thought she would be delighted to have a leisurely breakfast with Helen instead of slaving over the camper and the accompanying hassles of leaving.

"I've got a surprise for you!" I sang to Norma that morning.

She eyed me warily from behind her coffee cup.

"What's that?" she asked.

"I want you to go to breakfast with Helen while I pack the camper. Then, when you get back from breakfast, the camper will be ready and we can go!"

Well, she didn't think much of my idea at all. Instead, she bristled.

"Gary, you know that I always need to pack for myself," she said.

Being a woman of precise detail and order, she interpreted my offer as a "ploy" to get her out of my way so that I could pack the camper the way I wanted to. Of course, that was not my intention at all; I honestly had no secret motive. That she thought my innocent offer was some sort of scheme made me angry. I wanted to scream, "Okay, then, you pack the camper, and I'll go enjoy breakfast with Helen!"

Norma's suspicion had invalidated my loving offer and got our supposedly blissful camping trip off to a rocky start.

Now, let's replay the scene using drive-through listening. Instead of hurting my feelings with her negative interpretations, Norma could have used drive-through listening to establish my intentions.

I would've rushed into the kitchen, shouting, "I've got a surprise for you!" and then tell her my idea about her breakfasting with Helen while I packed the camper.

She could have taken time to *listen* to what I was saying and, instead of accusing me, she could have tried to understand me—by repeating what she'd thought she'd heard me say, just as a fast-food clerk repeats an order.

"Let me see if I'm hearing you correctly," she would have said. "You're saying you want to pack the camper. And you want me to go to breakfast with Helen. Then when I get back, it will all be done?"

"Yes, exactly!" I would have confirmed. "Tell me how you like that."

By asking her to tell me how she liked the idea in a non-threatening, nonaccusatory way, I would have initiated the drive-through listening method of communications. At this point, if she had suspicions of ulterior motives, she could also employ drive-through listening to ferret out the truth. "But are you really saying that you want me to get out of here so you can pack the camper the way you like it?" she could have said.

At that point, I could have told Norma that she, like the fast-food clerk, had gotten my "order" wrong.

"I'm feeling that you're only trying to get me out of the house so you can pack the camper any way you want," she would have said. But I wouldn't react to that line out of insecurity; I'd merely explain my true intention.

"No, that is not what I meant at all," I could have said. "I just wanted to make your life easier and give you the morning off."

If escalation begins, just take a time out and tell each other that you will revisit this issue later after you have both had a chance to calm down. Agree to try discussing the issue again later, this time using drive-through listening. You'll be amazed at your increased calm.

Employing drive-through listening almost instantly delivers you to the fourth and fifth levels of intimacy about our feelings and our needs, not bouncing back behind the wall through anger and defensiveness. You will avoid hurting each other. Drive-through listening—which, in relationship studies, has many names, including "reflective listening," the art of reflecting back to our mate what we think we've heard—allows you to leap the hurdles of invalidation and negative interpretations. It accomplishes this by using the back-and-forth of one partner's stating feelings and needs, then the other's restating those feelings and needs until both parties understand each other. Each back-and-forth burrows deeper into each other's feelings and needs, turning a simple conversation into a literal digging device with one direction: deeper understanding. Take turns being the clerk first and then letting your mate be the customer. Once you've made progress in your conversation, switch roles.

I realize it's hard to do this when you're feeling hurt. But remember: clerks at McDonald's and Burger King can use drive-through listening, even if they've had their feelings hurt by someone—which, of course, happens every day. So, come on! If high schoolers around the world can do it, you can control your emotions and pain for a few moments, too. At the same time, you must learn to see your mate's pain as a caution flag. If that pain has been caused by something you've said or done, it's wise to allow your mate to be the "customer" or speaker for the duration of the conversation, while you take the role of clerk or listening. Don't attempt to take turns in each role when one partner is feeling hurt. Just allow your mate to share his or her feelings about the pain. Take the "clerk," or listening role, and repeat the words back to your mate. It's not always easy to do, but it's the best technique for keeping the love and concern flowing. Later, when things calm down, ask if you can share what the "hurtful" experience did to you. But be careful that you don't escalate the hurt and reignite the situation.

But, of course, Norma and I didn't know any of this on the morning of our camping trip. So we hastily packed our camper together in silence. Then, nursing our separate emotional wounds, we drove off toward our campsite, abandoning the search for intimacy and speaking instead in cold clichés and empty facts.

These days, my wife, Norma, who runs our company, uses this method of communication daily with the male employees. She reminded me recently that she doesn't usually have to use it with the female staff—only the males—because it so effectively bridges understanding for the sexes. Recently, I witnessed her deftly wield this method of communication with a very tough owner of a publishing company during an extremely tense meeting. Even I was amazed at how calm the person became and we solved the problem in minutes.

Here are three main steps to learning to use drive-through listening:

1. Learn how to be the customer—the speaker in the car.
2. Learn how to be the fast-food employee—the listener inside the restaurant.
3. Learn how to resolve any differences or conflicts with solutions that give both partners a sense that they have "won" in the argument.

Learning to be a Customer (Speaker)

Now that I've defined what drive-through listening is, I can tell you how to use it specifically and practically to enhance your communication skills. First and foremost, proceed from a foundation of honor, placing your relationship with your mate above all earthly things. Remember that the highest form of honor is to consider your mate's needs and feelings just a little bit more important than your own. Then, begin the following exercises that I learned from the Bridging Interactive Seminars of Dr. Dallas and Nancy Demmitt. They call their mode of drive-through communication "discovery talking and listening." I've found it to be a highly effective framework that will assist you in thoroughly formulating your thoughts and feelings so that you may effectively talk about an issue from your point of view.

"Let's face it," write the Demmitts in the *Bridging Workshop* workbook. "So much has been bottled up inside of you over the years: feelings, events, strengths, desires, talents, joys, defeats, hurts, and fears. In addition to this, the differences and similarities between the various elements inside of you and the elements inside someone else, will either become the source of conflict or collaboration. The problem is, many of us haven't taken the time to investigate who we are and what we want . . . so we have difficulty expressing the true details of our heart to others. This adds to the conflict. . . . Others can't know what you are truly feeling inside unless you tell them. Likewise, you can't know the heart and mind of another unless they tell you."

In discovery talking (or "placing your order"), they have created a framework to assist in formulating your thoughts and feelings so you can speak to your mate from your point of view. For those of us who have faced important decisions but didn't know which way to turn, discovery talking can be an invaluable tool to uncover what you really want in your life and from your mate, and to discover what is motivating you in your desires. The Demmitts compare your dreams, desires, and values to "buried treasure" literally buried in your heart. Discovery talking is a tool to uncover that treasure and bring it into your world.

It is hoped you and your mate have already agreed to be LUVRs for each other—to Listen to one another, Understand each other, Validate your feelings and needs, Respect what you say, and Respond to feelings and needs with win-win solutions, as I explained in the last chapter.

Before You Begin: Cleaning Your Filters

Think of conversation as air coming through an air-conditioning system. Before it arrives clean, fresh, and cold in your living room, it has to pass through a cleansing filter, which you'll know if you've ever cleaned one can become blackened with soot, dirt, and impurities. Your conversation with your mate is the same way. Whatever you say passes through filters that, according to *Fighting for Your Marriage* by Markman, Stanley, and Blumberg, "change what goes through them. . . . A filter on a camera lens alters the properties of the light passing through it. A coffee filter lets the flavor through and leaves the grounds behind. As with any other filter, what goes in our communication filters is different from what comes out."

The authors hypothesize that we all "have many kinds of filters packed into our heads, which affect what we hear, what we say, and how we interpret things." The filters are created through years of experiences, thoughts, families, and cultural heritages.

Whenever we approach something new, unfamiliar, or unexpected, the wheels in our mind begin furiously spinning, attempting to find something familiar to place this new idea, experience, or action into a context. We use all of our history to try and help us identify this new happening in a familiar context. In other words, we try to place events in the box of our preconceptions. When we do this while communicating with our mates, the results can lead to snap judgments and gross misinterpretations.

Markman, Stanley, and Blumberg identify the different main filters that can hinder couples struggling to improve their communication skills: inattention, emotional states, beliefs and expectations, and differences in style. Let's discuss them one at a time.

Inattention

This is a common problem in a world where everyone has far too much on his or her plate: work schedules, family, and community responsibilities. We are constantly being distracted, by television, by telephones, by computers, by our children, by our superiors at work. It is difficult to have a calm and meaningful conversation when your mind is on five different subjects at any given moment. It's hard to stop, look, and listen when the telephone is ringing, the dog is barking, and the fax machine is beeping—all at the same maddening moment.

Inattention is caused not only by external forces such as the telephone but also by your internal agenda. Strapped for cash? Worried about your health or your children's welfare? At any given moment a thousand details are mentally calling you away from the conversation at hand. It's a fact that Americans are, as a whole, severely sleep deprived. We consume too much caffeine. We don't know what is healthy to eat anymore. We are torn between financial success and family success, and are confused over whether those two things are mutually exclusive. All the pressures of living are enough to keep us unfocused and diffused.

How does inattention act as a filter in conversation? Have you ever said something to someone and received the reply, "Huh? What did you say?" I certainly have and I was left frustrated, whether my listener meant any harm or not. When people don't pay attention to what you are saying, you feel invalidated, unimportant, insignificant. I bet you can name a hundred times when you tried to say something, only to be ignored. When your mate, friend, co-worker, or family member finally asked you what you wanted to say, you most likely spoke through your pain, saying, "Oh, just forget it."

When you are trying to make your relationship work, inattention can stop you at the starting gate. You cannot communicate if both parties are not *fully* participating, Once one of you feels invalidated, you can no longer speak at the fourth and fifth levels of intimacy—you can't share your feelings and needs. Nobody wants to tell you how he or she feels if you aren't going to listen. Let's study one conversation filtered through inattention:

> "Honey, I've been thinking . . ." says the wife.
>
> The husband, eyes glued to the football game on TV, replies, "Huh?"
>
> "We haven't had much time alone lately," she says.
>
> "Well, I had to work," he replies robotically.
>
> "I was hoping maybe we could schedule a weekend to spend together," she says. "Maybe go to the country or something, stay at a B&B. I could get Mom to watch the kids."
>
> "Aikman's gettin' ready to throw a pass!" he says, employing the filter of inattention.
>
> "Aren't you even listening to me?" she says, frustrated. "Oh, why do I even bother? It's obvious you don't care enough to even listen!"

This, of course, gets his attention, but by then it's too late. He's already blown the conversation by not being attentive in the first place. So he returns to the TV while she nurses her hurt feelings, and they drift further and further apart.

Emotional States

Your emotional state of mind is a filter that plays a major role in communication with your mate. If you're like most couples, you and your mate spend the majority of your days apart, working in separate locations or attending to separate errands and responsibilities. When you finally get together, you have all these individual experiences affecting your moods and in-terpretations. Something said in innocence could rub one of you the wrong way. Maintaining a good mood helps solve many a problem. Emotional states can either hurt or help, but they must be recognized in order to be disarmed.

The next time you are in a conversation with your mate and he or she snaps at you irrationally, storms out suddenly, or exhibits instant exasperation, consider that your mate is speaking or acting through the filter of his or her emotional state. Most likely, this emotional state is not wholly or even partially attributable to you. Ask if perhaps you should discuss the issue at a better time, or if your mate needs to get some-thing off his or her chest that is unrelated to the issue at hand.

Beliefs and Expectations

How you perceive your relationship will act as a filter in your communication. As Markman, Stanley, and Blumberg observe, "We 'pull' from others behavior that's consistent with what we expect." We often categorize our mate based on his or her characteristics, likes and dislikes, and personality traits, and we use our categorizations to interpret our mate's behavior. Sometimes our interpretations are accurate, but often they are not. We try to "mind read," but making assumptions about how someone else thinks or feels is a dangerous endeavor in our relationships. Instead of assuming, ask your mate how he or she feels. It will avoid miscommunication and open the doors to intimacy.

Differences in Style

By now, you are well aware that you and your mate have infi-nite differences. Chief among them are differences in your style of communication. You might be someone who opens your heart all the time, expresses every thought and every emotion, in order to feel satisfied. Your mate might be reserved and reticent. Like all your differences, your communication style arises from your personal history and background. Some families are very open and emotional—every issue might have been debated, sometimes through heated debate, even argument. Other families are very reserved. They resolve problems in soft voices, and any raising of the voice is considered inappropriate and unacceptable. You and your mate probably had different upbringings that influence how you handle problems in your own unique and different styles. Therefore, when your mate reacts in a way you do not know or understand, it can affect your interpretation of his or her intent or feelings.

There is, of course, one additional, perhaps most important, filter: self-protection. Think about it. In protecting their hearts from pain and rejection, many people erect filters, guarding against anything that might be or even appear painful. Sometimes, this filter of self-protection is so strong it also filters out any possibility of intimacy. You will literally guard your heart so carefully that nothing—good or bad—can break through. The filter of self-protection limits you from ever realizing the deepest levels with your mate.

All of these filters—inattention, emotional states, beliefs and expectations, differences in style, self-protection—will affect your exchanges with your mate. The consequence is that what your mate says and what you will actually hear in your head might be quite different. However, drive-through listening can eliminate filters and deliver you to the deepest levels of intimacy.

Rules for Placing Your Order

Before beginning this powerful exercise in the role of the speaker (the "customer"), remember to keep a few important concepts in mind:

1. The speaker's job is to express feelings or needs using "I" statements, as in "I'm trying to tell you that I need to

do something nice for you by packing the camper by myself."
You cannot bring up past issues, start a new argument, or
make blaming and accusatory "You" statements, as in "You
always . . ." "You never . . ." "You" statements like "You make
me mad . . . sad . . . etc." imply that you're a victim without
power or control over your own emotions and that the other
person is responsible for how you choose to react. This not
only adds to your sense of being "stuck," it calls for a defensive
reaction from your partner. To take responsibility for your
own feelings and reactions, change the statement to, "I'm
angry about" and describe the behavior that bothers you.

2. Do not focus blame and accusations on someone else.
Take full responsibility for your own feelings and needs. Others cannot "make" you feel a certain way; our choices produce
our own feelings. Explore the feelings and needs in your own
heart so a peaceful resolve can be found.

3. Ensure that you and your mate agree to avoid condemnation as each of you express what is in your hearts. Each of
you is entitled your own opinion, therefore speak openly about
the thoughts, pictures, and emotions that are coming to your
mind, so you can achieve the greatest degree of discovery and
healing. You must speak only for yourself. Do not try to read
the mind of your mate or judge your mate's thoughts.

4. Offer bite-sized thoughts or information so that the
other person can remember what you've said in order to repeat it back to you correctly and, ideally, understand your feelings and needs.

Relationship expert Hope E. Morrow has developed a
template for constructing "I" statements that can help you in
"placing your order" without hurt or anger. When you are trying to express a feeling, follow these four steps:

1. "I"
2. What you feel, need, or want
3. The event that evoked your feelings or desire (typically
something you both can agree on)
4. The effect the event has on you

Combine these pieces to form a sentence as follows: "I feel #2____ when #3____ , because #4____ ." For example, "(1) I feel (2) very scared (3) when you are late home from work, because (4) I worry something might have happened to you."

Avoid using statements that might imply that you are trying to mind-read or judge your mate. You can avoid this by concentrating on your own feelings and unmet needs. Take ownership of what is yours, not your mate's. Try not to use "We" statements—"We're always fighting," "We can't understand each other"—which usually involve one person's speaking for another without permission or agreement, inviting defensiveness and potential anger from the other.

Also, when you are expressing your emotions, don't downplay your negative feelings. It is common to try and suppress your anger when you first use "I" statements. But when you minimize the intensity of your feelings, you make less of an impact on your listener, and his or her response might not satisfy you. Be honest about the intensity of your feelings so that you and your mate can deal with them. Be careful, when expressing anger, to emphasize love, concern, and disappointment rather than dishonor. Saying, "I feel very angry about your inattention," is honest and direct. Saying, "I feel like you are a jerk," is not constructive.

Using Discovery Talking

As the "customer," the speaker, you will need to learn the most effective way of communicating your feelings and needs. The Demmitts call this "discovery talking" because both you and your listener will make "discoveries" when you use it well. Not only will your mate begin to understand how you feel and what you need but *you* will be able to better define those feelings and needs as well. It's not just your mate who can misinterpret your emotions—it's you, too! You will soon see what I mean.

Keep in mind that, in the examples that follow, I am using an average couple who has an average amount of honor, love, and conflict in their relationship. Later, we will discuss how more conflicted couples can use drive-through listening.

First, choose an issue that is important to you at this moment. An "issue" can be loosely defined as something that concerns you. It could be anything—your home, your job, your relationship, a behavior pattern you'd like to change, or a decision you have to make. Now, begin using the Demmitts' discovery talking skills to resolve your issue.

Discovery Talking Skill 1:
What I See and Hear

Okay, as the speaker, you're in your car, reading the take-out menu. Let's say the issue on your mind is your mate's increasing distance and apparent inability to communicate with you. Instead of jumping into an accusatory inquisition, demanding from your mate an explanation for his or her "wrong" behavior, try a different tactic. Start a conversation with an observation rather than an accusation. State only what you have physically seen or heard, with no interpretation attached.

In my example, a wife is concerned over her increasingly distant husband who arrives home from work, eyes cast down, jaw clenched, and voice silent. The wife has two choices: she can either avoid the issue or confront it. In discovery talking, you address the issue by beginning with observations, the communications technique of merely stating what you've seen or heard.

"I notice you're not smiling," she says. "I see your eyes looking down at the ground and I don't hear you saying anything." That observation made, you can move quickly to the next skill.

Discovery Talking Skill 2:
What I Think

The human brain is an immensely complex piece of machinery, but in many ways it is quite predictable. Once you receive information—as the wife received the image of her distraught and distant husband—your brain begins the process of giving meaning to what you've seen or heard. Your mind goes to work forming an "opinion"—that dangerous form of thought that can slam you against the wall of conflict if you start expressing the opinion through accusation.

The wife mentioned above could have immediately voiced her opinions of why she believed her husband was angry. She might convince herself that it's all her fault, that he doesn't love her . . . and this assumption could certainly turn an issue into an argument.

At this point, stop, look, and listen. Once you've formed an opinion, don't voice it as accusation! Put your opinion into the framework of what you are thinking, once again employing "I" language.

"I notice you're not smiling," says the wife. "I see your eyes looking down at the ground and I don't hear you saying anything." To this statement, she adds her opinion, framed in nonthreatening "I" language: "I am wondering if you are mad at me," she says.

It's very simple, yet it gets to the heart of the issue at hand. She has brought the hidden thoughts and theories she has formulated into the light, instead of letting them fester.

Now, she's ready to tell her husband how she feels.

The overall goal of drive-through listening is to help create a safe place to share the deepest levels of intimacy with each other. The safer and more valued you feel, the deeper you'll allow your mate look into your heart. While you are learning to use this method, remember to help your mate feel comfortable as you move forward. Intimacy can feel awkward in the beginning. For example, I own an American Standard horse. It's an Amish horse, the kind you usually see pulling a buggy. Today I moved two cows and my horse into a new pasture. It was a simple move, but it took me almost an hour because the animals were very nervous about what I was trying to do with them. I had to move very slowly and use food to goad them, but eventually they reached their destination. Likewise, your mate may need some gentle help, support, and direction in learning these skills. A little tenderness goes a long way.

Discovery Talking Skill 3:
What I Feel

Sharing feelings is, of course, the fourth level of intimacy. But according Dallas and Nancy Demmitt, thoughts combined with feelings "will do to emotions what a match will do to the dry kindling—just a spark and the inferno is set ablaze! How you interpret different situations will affect what you feel about them (and, if you have acquired a wrong interpretation, it can lead you to a flood of misplaced feelings!)"

In the case of a wife facing an emotionally distant husband, her initial feeling would probably be hurt and resentment. Add to this equal parts pain, fear, and anxiety about her future. Denying or delaying addressing these issues won't make them go away. No, just the opposite will occur! Her feelings will turn to anger and, potentially, rage. She will think "How can he treat me like this!" and the emotions will whirl around her until she feels caught in a mental cyclone. She will become unable to feel joy. She may be unable to trust people. She could fall prey to self-destructive feelings and behavior and begin numbing herself with food, drugs, or alcohol.

It helps if she conveys her feelings to her husband, using "I" language. "I notice you aren't smiling," she might say. "I saw your eyes looking down at the ground and I don't hear you saying anything [what she sees and hears] . . . I am wondering if you are mad at me [what she thinks] . . . I feel anxious about the way things appear . . . and I am annoyed that you aren't speaking up!"

That nails it. She has conveyed her feelings, not only in one way but two, as being both "anxious" and "annoyed." Pay special attention to the words she is using. She is putting her feelings into the simplest possible form, using the words "I am" as much as possible. It's the best way to describe a feeling to your mate: instead of exhaustively explaining your feelings—which can result in misunderstanding—keep it simple, three words whenever possible: "I am angry." "I am worried." "I am scared."

To help you tap into your feelings on any issue, the Dem-mitts devised four "feelings" categories, suggesting that you become familiar with each of them. To discover your thoughts, feelings, and emotions on whatever issue you're grappling with, complete the following four sentences.

"I'm fearful that . . ."
"I'm angry about . . ."
"I'm sad about . . ."
"I'm ashamed or sorry about . . ."

Once you're clear on where you stand, you're ready to move into the next vital skill of discovery talking.

Discovery Talking Skill 4:
What I Want or Need

Once you know and express to your mate what you've seen or heard, what you think and how you feel, you might be surprised to see where this process leads you. Expressing your thoughts and feelings instead of denying or delaying them will take you to an almost majestic place: you'll almost automatically know what you want.

Still, desires can be difficult. Because we all desire many things at once, some of our desires may conflict with each other. Therefore, instead of blurting our your desires all at once—which could confuse and frustrate both you and your mate—you must learn to categorize them into three parts: (1) what you want for yourself; (2) what you want for the person with whom you are in conflict; and (3) what you want for the two of you together.

Notice the language the Demmitts are using. They're not suggesting that you discover what you want "from" your mate, but what you want "for" them, for yourself and for the two of you together. Wanting something "for" someone is different from what you want from them. "From" is a one-sided word; it involves your mate's giving and your taking. Wanting "for" someone is the essence of mutual give and take.

In the case of a wife facing a distraught husband, she might divide her three desires the following way:

- *Her desire for herself.* "I want to know what's bothering my husband, so I won't feel so anxious."
- *Her desire for her husband.* "I want him to get some relief from what might be bothering him."
- *Her desire for her and her husband.* "I want us to have a pleasant evening together."

Now that she has expressed what she's seen or heard, what she thinks, how she feels, and what she wants, the process of back-and-forth, of drive-through listening, can begin. How far you take this process depends on you and your mate. The deeper you both go to investigate the desires of your heart, the more you can confess and convey your feelings and needs to each other.

Here is an exercise to help you practice the skill of discovery talking.

1. Divide a sheet of paper into four equal parts. At the top of the page write down the "issue" you and your mate are discussing. Label each of the four sections as follows: "See/Hear," "Think," "Feel," and "Want." Leave room for both you and your mate to fill in information about how you feel, think, and want about the topic. Here are the questions to answer: "What do I see and hear?" "What do I think it means?" "What do I feel?" "What do I want for the other person involved?"

2. On another sheet of paper, you and your mate should write out the issue you're facing and describe it in the detail you would reserve for writing a story. Make the issue come alive on the page. Be specific and write out every detail concerning the issue. Choose an issue that concerns both of you, then take turns reading what you've written about the issue at hand.

3. When reading, one person should be designated the "reader," the other the "listener." Let the reader read! The listener's turn to express what he or she thinks was seen/heard, thinks, feels, and wants comes only when the reader is finished reading. The one exception is when a listener feels over-

whelmed by too much information at once. In that case, if you are the listener, try to gently interrupt—perhaps by a hand gesture—and tell your reader that you need to try and paraphrase smaller amounts of information. Try to summarize what you have already heard, then urge your reader to continue. Do not ask questions. Only paraphrase and give the spotlight back to the reader.

Learning to Be a Good Clerk (Listener)

Speaking, of course, is only half of the equation. To communicate in the deepest levels of intimacy requires listening, too. As we discussed before, hearing is perhaps the most mighty, yet most misunderstood, of our five senses. Listening can help you avoid misunderstanding and conflict, reduce false assumptions, stop the natural tendency to react in the panic or crisis mode, and reduce fear, loneliness, and pain. As the Demmitts write: "Just by showing someone that you are willing to listen—without condemning or judging them—will help to make that person feel valued, loved, honored, and appreciated."

To learn the power of discovery listening, you'll have to begin with one vow: to rid yourself of what the Demmitts call the "How-can-I-get-you-to-shut-up-and-listen-to-me?" mindset and replace it with a "What-can-I-do-to-create-a-safe-place-where-understanding-can-take-root-and-grow?" attitude.

Here's their easy-to-follow path to discovery listening:

Think of listening as creating a safe place for your mate to speak. In this place you will not seek ways to attack what he or she is saying. You will not turn around what your mate says in order to advise, punish, teach, or lecture him or her. Finally, you will paraphrase what you believe your mate said, without coloring your repetition with your own opinions of ideal outcomes and judgments. Even if your mate goes on the attack—with accusations and blame—you will not react, but merely hear them out. You will put yourself into "neutral" by remembering that what's important in listening is not what you want to say, but hearing what your mate is trying to tell you. Your goal is to lead your mate into the "safe place" for communication, where true intimacy begins to deepen and grow. It's like when I led my horse into the new pasture . . . just take it slow and easy.

When receiving an "order," you must repeat back only what you've heard. You cannot edit, evaluate, or defend yourself. You can ask to have the order repeated if you didn't understand something. However, this is only for clarity, not for agreement or disagreement. You are merely trying to understand what your mate is saying. Don't worry about whether or not you agree with statements as you listen, or whether you will somehow be cheated if you agree to take a new direction that your mate suggests. One of the points of drive-through listening is to find solutions that will make both you and your mate feel like winners.

By giving your mate the gift of listening, you will earn the right to speak at a later time. But first "anchor" yourself to listen. Sit down with your mate, close your mouth, and open your ears . . . and prepare yourself to experience the power of discovery listening.

Discovery Listening Skill 1:
Focus on the Other Person

Anchoring yourself to listen means giving your mate your full and complete attention. Here are a few ways to do it:

- *Open posture.* Face your mate. If you are sitting, turn your chairs toward each other and then relax. Unfold your arms and your legs—as folded appendages send a subliminal message of being "on guard" or "closed-minded." Unfolding your appendages sends a signal that you are letting down your guard and literally welcoming your mate inside your space.
- *Encouraging nods and acknowledging words.* You must let your mate know that you're focused on what he or she is saying. All it takes is an occasional nod or a word—just a single word!—of affirmation, as simple as "Yes," "Uh-huh," or "I see."
- *Eye contact.* During one of the Demmitts' workshops, a

wife told her husband, "When you look at me while I'm talking it's like you are touching me with your eyes." What a powerful mode of unspoken conversation! Making eye contact with your mate is the quickest and easiest way to say, "I'm interested in what you're saying." Eye contact is, of course, one of the directions on the ultimate relationship roadmap. In her book *You Just Don't Understand*, Deborah Tannen cites research in which children were given a subject to discuss. The little boys didn't look at each other as they spoke; they sat side-by-side and stared into space. However, the little girls turned their chairs toward each other and watched each other with full attention as they conversed. This behavior continued through childhood and young adulthood. Its meaning? Men must learn to focus most on maintaining eye contact.

• *Touch.* This is the most powerful nonverbal listening skill, the way to immediately drain anger from a situation. Just try it. I think you'll discover that when you touch your mate while you listen—holding hands, knees touching, a pat on the back—you will find it hard to focus on anger. But remember that this does not mean anything that could be remotely considered a sexual touch, which can ignite anger and unleash pain when you're dealing with an unresolved issue.

• *Set the scene.* Eliminating distractions is paramount to discovery listening. Turn off the TV, unplug the phone. Make arrangements for the kids. Let your mate know that listening is more important than anything else to you at this moment.

Now that you're ready to listen, truly listen, here's the path to follow:

Discovery Listening Skill 2: Summarize the Other Person

This essence of drive-through listening allows you to avoid the traps of misunderstanding. The best way to summarize is not to "repeat" every word like a tape recorder, but to break down bits of what you're hearing your mate say into bite-sized pieces, then to paraphrase to your mate these pieces when they're finished with each statement.

Begin by saying "What I hear you saying . . ." or "You're feeling that . . ." or "You are wanting . . ." Then, summarize what you think he or she is trying to tell you without coloring your response with your own interpretations.

You're honoring your mate by allowing him or her to be the final authority on what he or she is saying. Here is where I saw my wife Norma really use this method. A businessman was climbing all over me during a conference call, making what I considered to be unfounded allegations, which immediately set me off on the all-too-typical rout of rage. Norma and I listened, and initially I began to react to his accusations. I was just about ready to begin verbally punching when Norma began using her drive-through listening skills.

Norma started paraphrasing everything the man was saying. She was calm and direct. "Is this what you are saying . . . ?" she would say. He would respond and say more, and she just kept summarizing and restating what he was saying until he stopped and calmed down. Even I calmed down! It was amazing. Then she suggested a solution, completely based on how she had listened to his concerns. He liked the solution. We hung up and never had to address this issue with the businessman again. Norma had been able to suggest that solution because she had really concentrated on his words and understood his needs in this situation. There's not a week that goes by that we don't use this method at work with someone.

Now, what do you do if what your speaker is saying is too long to summarize? Merely hold up your hand to stop and say something like, "Please let me understand you." Then, paraphrase what you've heard up to this point. I understand that this process may seem a bit infantile at first, but could it be any more childlike than blowing up or storming out? You might think paraphrasing what your mate is saying tells your mate that you haven't heard what he or she has said, but this is just conditioning. The conventional view is to let the speaker drone on until finished—or to combat at every turn. But allowing your mate to ramble only leads to confusion and conflict.

So summarize what you hear your mate saying every couple of sentences without adding your own interpretations.

Then, allow your mate to agree or disagree with what you've told him or her you've heard. Your mate may correct you! Or your mate might say, "That's right. That's exactly what I mean." This is what you're seeking—the "That's right!" response. Sometimes, your summary will result in your mate's understanding what he or she is trying to say more clearly. Your listening becomes a gift through which your mate can actually understand more about him- or herself or discover a deeper issue that the words are trying to convey.

If this happens, if your mate even expresses shame or shock about what he or she has said and how you've heard it, then your mate may begin questioning him or herself, asking, "How could I have allowed this to happen?" When these questions arise, don't answer or lecture them! Continue to listen and to paraphrase and restate what you've heard. This gives the speaker the opportunity to answer his or her own questions and show you the inner terrain of his or her heart.

Always remember: your rapt attention is more encouraging than anything you can say.

Discovery Listening Skill 3:
Invite the Other Person to Say More

Now, when he or she is speaking, your mate is most likely going to pause, perhaps to gather his or her thoughts, perhaps just to take a breath, perhaps a momentary break before what your mate really wants to say is unveiled. But this seemingly simple pause could be a test. By pausing, your mate might be checking to see if you are truly listening. Do not fall into the trap of thinking that the pause is an invitation for you to speak. If you do, you're likely to derail your mate's train of conversation and, more important, his or her trust.

Every instance of discovery listening is a search for buried treasure, the secret truths that stand the chance of being exposed . . . if you will truly listen. What comes behind that "pause" may be the most important part of what your mate is trying to say. Do not undermine the discovery of this treasure by breaking in with your own statements.

Simply ask, if the pause continues too long, "Anything more?" or "Is there anything else you want me to know or understand?" This is akin to saying, "Would you like anything else with your order?" or "Would you like fries with that?"

You may have to ask this question repeatedly before your mate responds, especially if the pause is because what comes after the pause is uncomfortable to say. But restrain yourself; keep your response to those three little words, "Is there more?" You'll be surpassed at how those three words can lead your mate to express feelings and needs, taking your relationship to the deepest levels of intimacy.

Discovery Listening Skill 4:
Ask the Other Person Questions

Once you understand what your mate is trying to say, but he or she still doesn't know how to use what he or she has said to help him or herself, you can ask leading questions for further discovery.

Asking the right questions at a nonthreatening time can lead your mate into deeper terrain of the heart and brain, just as asking the wrong question at a threatening time can derail the conversation and lead to immediate conflict. Remember that change will come only when your mate speaks and understands what he or she is expressing, not when you try and speak for the person or convince him or her. Your mate must come to his or her own conclusion and your gift of listening is a platform on which to exhibit feelings and needs—and to see them clearly. You can guide your mate, but you cannot decide for your mate.

Here are four invaluable lessons on asking your mate guiding questions:

1. *When to ask.* Ask the question after you've completed summarizing one of your mate's bite-sized statements. How will you know when you're finished summarizing? When you ask your mate, "Is there more?" he or she will say, "No. That's it. You've got it right."

2. *How you ask.* Before you begin asking questions, ask for permission simply by asking, "May I ask you a question?" It's a small courtesy, but it can have enormous results. Asking questions can be irritating; it can be construed as an invasion of privacy. Allow your mate to have the right to say, "No, I'd rather you not ask a question now." More than likely, however, your mate will be thankful for your request and say, "Yes, please go ahead." If the answer is "Not now," however, heed the warning. Stop asking and keep listening.

3. *Ask open questions.* Avoid what I call dead-end questions that end with yes or no. Dead-end questions give the listener only two choices. To avoid these types of questions, begin with the words "what," how," "when," or "where," as in "How do you feel?" "When did this begin?"

4. *Avoid "Why" questions.* Beginning a question with the word "why" can seem accusatory. "Why do you act like that? "Why can't you . . ." "Why aren't you. . . ?" Your mate will go on the defensive and your communication will shut down in a hurry.

Remember, always stick to your role as either speaker or listener. You can stop an argument your mate may be pushing you toward by showing that you will only be the clerk (the listener). If you stick to this role and avoid expressing your opinions, concerns, or expectations, your mate cannot escalate the argument.

Here is how it works:

YOUR MATE: *"You're always late and I'm sick of it!"*
YOUR SUMMARY: *"You want me to know you're more than upset; you've reached your limit with me?"*
YOUR MATE: *"Yes, and I've had it!"*
YOUR RESPONSE: *"Say more!"*
YOUR MATE: *"Well, be on time for once."*
YOUR SUMMARY: *"You want me to be on time for once. Is there anything else bothering you about me being late?"*
YOUR MATE: *"Yes. I work hard to be on time for you, but you don't seem to care about wasting my time."*

YOUR SUMMARY: *"So, when I am late, it makes you feel like I don't care enough about you to be on time?"*
YOUR MATE: *"Yes! That's it!"*

Drive-Through Listening Rules to Remember

1. Decide your roles. One person must be the listener and one must be the speaker. Whoever is the speaker has the floor without exception until he or she is finished stating feelings. When that speaker is finished, the roles will be switched, giving the other mate the floor. This way, you will both have your chance to speak. You both understand this in the beginning. So instead of fighting for the floor, you will start off with the unspoken agreement that you'll be sharing it as equals.

2. The listener must invite the "order." In the case of our misunderstood camper fiasco, Norma was the speaker and I became the listener merely because, if I'd been familiar with drive-through, I would have initiated the order by starting off with, "OK, please tell me how you feel. I want to listen and understand." It's up to you to initiate drive-through by taking the listener position—and all you have to do is say, "Tell me how you feel." Be sincere—show your full attention, make eye contact, and try to make physical contact—by holding your mate's hand, touching his or her knee or shoulder.

3. The speaker then must express his or her feelings or needs in the current conflict. In Norma's case, she would have answered my question, "How do you feel?" with her belief that I was merely trying to get her out of the house so I could pack the camper my way. As a speaker, you must avoid accusations; instead, use "I" statements to tell your mate how you feel. Your purpose should be to help the listener understand how you feel about the issue at hand. Avoid bringing up events from the past or starting a new argument. Do not try to speak for your mate; do not try to "mind read." Express only your feelings, concerns, and needs.

4. As the speaker, try to convey your feelings one at a time. Giving too much information at once may cause the listener to miss something and not understand the "order." Don't

rush—you will have enough time to get out everything you want your mate to know.

5. The listener should paraphrase the speaker, making sure he or she understands the "order" clearly and without judgment ("You're saying you feel that I'm trying to get you out of the house so I can pack the camper any way I want?"). There is no room for evaluation in this exercise. The listener's goal is to show his or her mate that the listener is giving the issue full attention and wants to honor his or her feelings and needs. It is essential that you both have this back-and-forth conversation without judgment and that both of you understand that each party's feelings and needs are valid. Listeners cannot evaluate, edit, or defend themselves. They must simply listen and repeat.

6. Only when the speaker feels heard and validated do you switch roles.

7. Don't try to problem-solve while the speaker is talking and the listener is paraphrasing. You will have time to resolve issues later. The primary goal is to feel heard and understood and to feel that you have heard and understood. You are giving each other the gift of listening.

8. Summarizing statements in the listener role does not mean you agree with what's being said. Instead, the goal is to listen and validate the other person's feelings and individuality.

9. Throughout the drive-through process, remember that you are not looking for solutions, but understanding. Solutions can be sought after each person feels heard and validated.

10. Agree to take a time out if you see any of the four divorce factors—withdrawal, escalation, invalidation or negative beliefs—creeping into the conversation.

11. Above all else, strive to honor one another in all that is said and repeated!

One word of caution: do not begin practicing drive-through listening with a sensitive or controversial topic, especially something that is painful from your past. Optimum conversation is a process and you'll want to begin gradually and move forward as you feel comfortable. Begin with less volatile conflicts like being late for dinner or other "minor" grievances. As your skills increase in using drive-through listening, you'll naturally feel safer to use it with more serious and sensitive matters.

Begin gradually and don't rush the process—and remember always that drive-through is a process, not something that you try once and then stop. It will work wonders, but you have to dedicate yourself to the process. If you can enter into the process with a spirit of honor by merely listening and repeating what you've heard, you will provide your mate with a safe environment in which to express and discuss feelings and needs. In such an environment, any anger dissipates quickly. When someone is listening to you with great concern and valuing who you are, anger is reduced and easily drains away. Once each of you feels heard, understood, and validated, you can begin to look for permanent solutions, instead of pushing for minor, petty, temporary victories.

Yes, drive-through listening can be an easy practice to perfect. But there is one big obstacle that will constantly attempt to trip you up. You'll need to consider it with each word you speak. You must be on guard for the elements that can cause you to misinterpret and misunderstand your mate: your individual filters.

Putting Your Words to Work

Now, let's use the skills we've learned to communicate, really communicate, with our mates. The first step is to honor, to mentally lift up your mate above all earthly things. Then, lay down your emotional armor, your opinions, blame, condemnation, all negativity. And reduce every potentially negative thought, impression, or interpretation to ashes with honor.

Ask your mate to join you in a conversation.

Set a time limit for your discussion.

Then, sit down with your mate, facing one another in chairs. Uncross your arms and legs, look your mate squarely in the eyes, and then invite the order, saying, "I really want to listen to what is going on with you. Help me understand. I will listen to whatever you want to talk about."

Remember, you've taken on the role of listener merely by inviting the order. Your mate is the speaker. Your job is to listen, really listen, and to learn lessons from what you've learned and to paraphrase, in bite-sized chunks, what you've heard.

Let's review and summarize the skills of discovery listening and, as the speaker, discovery speaking.

As the Listener

1. Focus completely on the speaker through open posture, eye contact, and touch; eliminate distractions.
2. Summarize, then repeat back to your mate, his or her statements without interpretation.
3. Invite your mate, through nonthreatening, nonaccusatory prompting, to say more.
4. Ask permission to ask questions, then use guiding questions to clarify what your mate needs to resolve the issue.

As the Speaker

1. Pick an issue and tell your mate what you see and hear about it.
2. Ensure that you and your mate both agree on what the topic for discussion is going to be.
3. Tell your mate what you think.
4. Tell your mate how you feel.
5. Tell your mate what you want.

Once you've moved through this process a few times, I think you'll be surprised at the results. You'll eventually look up from one of your drive-through conversations and see that it has achieved a palpable power of propulsion, the simple act of speaking and listening will have delivered you deeper understanding and intimacy. You'll find yourself telling each other, "If we would have had this conversation a year ago, we could have saved ourselves such grief!"

Getting to the "Aha" Moment: Finding Win-Win Solutions

Now, you're ready to search for win-win solutions to whatever problem you might be facing as a couple. It takes work, but solutions will come, and not in a subtle manner. Solutions will become amazingly apparent, roaring in like sunlight breaking through curtains in a darkened room, and you'll be startled at how simple they are. Therapists call it the "aha" moment, and Dallas and Nancy Demmitt call it "Going for the cookie." It's when everything becomes clear.

Here are a few key aspects to focus upon:

1. Look for solutions only after both of you have had a chance to be heard, understood, and validated. Don't seek solutions until you've run the drive-through process, each of you playing both roles, as speaker and listener.

2. Remember that a one-sided solution is no solution at all. Once you've run the drive-through process, take turns offering solutions to the problem. Call a truce before you begin; say to each other, "There are no wrong ideas. So let's think of whatever comes to mind. The wilder, the better! And no matter what comes out, we're not going to get mad at each other. No judging! Anything goes!"

3. Once the potential solutions arise, write them down. Then, begin evaluating them. Narrow down your list to the best three to five solutions.

4. Finally, choose the solution you like best and try it for awhile. Schedule a time to reconvene to determine whether it's working or not. If it's not working, move on to the next best solution on your list.

5. If no solution becomes clear, continue using drive-through listening until a solution hits both of you as a winner.

Take the fact that no solution has occurred as a sign that you need to continue communicating.

Once you master the skill of ultimate conversation, of drive-through listening, you will have arrived at the place where intimacy is eternal. Now, it's time to learn how to stay in the deepest levels of intimacy by recharging your mate daily through love.

CHAPTER SEVEN

Recharging Your Mate's "Needs Battery" Through Love

Skill Number 3

Top Seven Love Needs

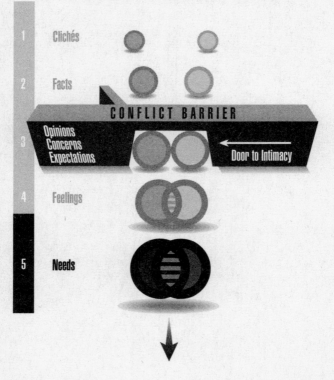

SO HERE WE ARE at the deepest level of intimacy. It's not a place of celebration, but an area requiring even more work: discovering and meeting the most important needs of your mate. As relationship expert and author Stephen Covey says, "Every major conflict between couples is the result of someone's needs not being met." Let's begin with a story from my marriage.

If conflicts are mainly caused by a mate's needs or emotions being misunderstood, neglected, or invalidated, I should have foreseen major fight between my wife and me a few months ago. Norma has an essential need to have order and rules obeyed in her life. One of the set of rules she lives by is the process by which she cares for her clothes. Norma has, over the years, accumulated a small wardrobe of "special" outfits that she treats with particular care. She washes them in the machine, then lets them only gently "fluff" in the dryer for a few moments before she hangs them from a special line in our laundry room to let them dry by air.

One day I was in the laundry room attending to a few of my own things when I saw her clothes had finished a cycle in the washing machine. Thinking that I could do her a favor, maybe give her a little TLC, I placed Norma's clothes in the dryer, intending to fluff them for five minutes and hang them as she usually does. Unfortunately, things didn't go according to plan. I got distracted by a phone call and forgot about the clothes—until about an hour later, when I went in to retrieve my own things. *Oops!* I had dried a whole load of her "special" clothes for way too long, and they had shrunk to miniature size.

Even with the best of intentions, I had neglected to meet one of Norma's most important needs: to always follow the rules. In drying her clothes the wrong way, I had not followed her rules, and as a result, some of her most prized possessions were ruined. I felt terrible, and I knew she would feel even worse—and for good reason!

I had a decision to make. How could I tell Norma about how I had neglected her clothing without ruining her day, her week, her year? One thought did occur to me: why not put all her things back in the washer and send them through the regular wash cycle again? Then, she would find them later and fuss at the washer instead of me. I could just hear it: "Gary, we need a new washer!" Instead, I started up the stairs like a dead man walking. "Norma?" I called weakly.

"Yes?" she replied from the bedroom.

Lamely I stood before her, one hand clutching a silk mini-blouse behind my back and out of her sight. I decided to try using humor to ease her inevitable anger. "I have good news, and I have bad news," I said.

Norma's brow furrowed. "What is the bad news?" she asked.

"Well," I said with a deep breath, "I wanted to do something special for you, so I tried to dry your clothes. But wait! There's good news: Our granddaughter Taylor now has a whole new wardrobe."

Norma's eyes grew to the size of saucers as I revealed the ruined blouse. She certainly wasn't happy—by neglecting her need for order and process, my well-intentioned "favor" had ruined half her wardrobe. Now we were thrust into the fifth level of intimacy whether we liked it or not.

I stared at her desperately. I felt incredibly embarrassed. "I'm sorry, Norma. I knew how you wanted them to dry, but I got distracted, and . . ." I paused and hung my head. "I'm really sorry."

Norma, saint that she is, knew that at that moment, my greatest need was forgiveness. "I know you didn't mean to do it," she finally said, sadly taking the rumpled silk in her hand and granting me a weak but genuine smile. "It's all right."

"We could go shopping if you would like," I offered brightly.

"OK," she agreed, and I knew we were okay.

"But I'm warning you, this stuff took me a long time to find!" she added.

By being honest about the situation, I had made a tough situation easier. Likewise, Norma had kept her calm and reason even in her disappointment. I had unwittingly ignored one of her needs, but I had tried to make up for it by meeting another of her needs: for me to acknowledge the importance of what she holds dear and to admit my mistake. In turn, she had met my need for attachment to others by drawing from her unconditional love for me.

The Deepest Level of Intimacy

This story illustrates the fact that the deepest level of love is not some fantasyland, not some pink-and-blue, satin-lined gift box, not an absolutely, everlastingly perfect world. No, the deepest level of intimacy takes hard work to discover and even harder work to maintain. But if you understand what it takes to have the loving relationship you desire and you apply that knowledge, steadfastly believing that the work you do will not be in vain, *you will see results.* And the results will motivate you and provide you with more and more energy to maintain a better relationship.

The deepest level of intimate communication is a wondrous world of understanding and sharing, of gut-level, back-and-forth interaction. Here, you will feel safe enough to share your most **important needs,** and you will know that your mate will listen and understand your uniqueness. The fifth level of intimacy, the deepest level of communication, involves first discovering the most important needs to be met in your relationship, then devising a plan to meet each other's needs. But to stay in the deepest level, you and your mate must become mutual masters of meeting your most important individual needs. Only in meeting these needs can you truly become one and remain in the deepest level of love.

Remember the distant dentist and his frustrated wife discussed earlier in this book? The couple who exiled themselves to a lifetime of sharing cold, bland facts about their shared occupation in dentistry? Remember how the panicked dentist, finding his wife's bags packed and her mind set on leaving, sounded the 911 alarm, which sent me rushing into their living room? When I encouraged her to paint a word picture about the state of their marriage in terms he could understand, she said that their marriage was like a potentially fatal dental infection and the infection was about ten inches away from her heart. The wife had come to the end of her emotional rope; but it wasn't simply her husband's actions that took her there. It was his *inaction* in not recognizing and fulfilling her basic needs. She was literally a 911 case of unrecognized and unfulfilled needs! She desperately needed her husband to slow down his 100 mph lifestyle and spend some quality time with her developing a real relationship connection—or she was heading out the door.

Her husband had his own set of needs, of course—the overriding need for accomplishment, success, and acclaim, to be valued for who he is and what he does. His needs were being met, although most of them from outside of the marriage. It was a classic case. He was the strong partner, the dominant partner. Their needs became a tug-of-war in which the stronger partner (the husband) always won. In the estimated daily hour-and-a-half that most couples interact because of work and kids, they'd wrestle over their conflicting needs. But, as always, his controlling personality would be fulfilled while her less aggressive needs were left to fester. However, in this case as in most, the mate with unmet needs eventually finds a way to get recognized—and it's usually amid the sound of slamming doors, snapping suitcases, and tires squealing out of driveways.

These scenarios—the kind that lead directly to separation and divorce—are most always the result of unmet needs. In the case of the dentist and his wife, it was obvious that he didn't understand her simple basic need for attention and affection, and so he couldn't meet his wife's needs from her viewpoint. Maybe he heard her endless attempts to express her needs, but he didn't understand the critical importance of what she'd been telling him. To him, his wife's pleas for attention were background noise, something to deal with "someday." But with her bags packed and the relationship consultant in his living room, his "someday" had arrived with a bang.

What We Cannot Live Without

There are yearnings that we will literally do anything to meet. Just like the physical needs of water, air, and food, human beings have emotional needs that must be fulfilled. It is the simple magic of a touch, the poetry of a kiss, the majesty of deep and honest conversation that constitute the essential moments of our lives. The need for companionship in a longlasting relationship is so strong that men and women will go to any length to satisfy it. And if marriage isn't meeting their needs, they may go outside the marriage and into an emotional or sexual affair.

Our needs are inextricably tied to our psychological makeup. If we're thwarted in having our need for real, emotional companionship met, emotional problems can arise: depression, passive aggression, learned helplessness, even suicide. We will even make up unreal situations to compensate for the deep need for companionship we lack. Humans will find a way to meet their needs at work or play, and with relatives, friends, children, or in the community at large.

But millions of people the world over never understand their mate's needs. This was certainly the case of the absent dentist of our earlier story. He didn't understand the depth of his wife's needs until she decided that the only route to fulfillment was in leaving him.

In the living room that day, I asked his wife a single question:

"What would it take to save this marriage?"

When she replied that all her husband had to do was spend quality time with her and their children, she wasn't speaking strictly from intellect; she was speaking from her heart. She was sharing her deepest needs: the need to connect with her mate through conversation, the need to be together as a family. In that instance, she was speaking from the deepest level of intimacy, even though her husband had yet to join her there. She was giving him directions into her heart.

Now, when his wife says, "We need to talk," the dentist hears the statement as a need, instead of a fleeting desire or a nag, a requirement as adamant as if she said, "I'm suffocating and need some oxygen—fast!" He has learned to recognize his wife's needs and to take the time to tend to those needs on a daily basis. This simple recognition, and subsequent action, has taken this once-distant couple, at the doorway of separation and perhaps divorce, into the deepest level of intimacy, which is best described as understanding and meeting each other's needs.

Here's how you can get there—and stay there.

Learning to Wield the Life Force of Love

The first law of fulfilling needs is to realize that everyone's are different, based on personalities, backgrounds, and expectations. So you must first learn to recognize your mate's individual needs, as well as your own.

You might be surprised at what you discover. I know I was. Having no knowledge of basic emotional needs back then, I relied on happenstance discoveries in my own life and marriage. Pretty soon, a pattern emerged. I discovered that I have a need to connect with people. My wife has a need to be by herself. I have a need to verbalize what I'm thinking. My wife has the need to process what she hears before speaking. During vacations, I have a need for spontaneity. She has a need for making and sticking to plans.

Because we didn't understand each other's needs in the beginning. Norma and I frequently found ourselves frustrated. When she discouraged me from always verbalizing my thoughts, I'd feel constricted, almost ready to explode. If she said, "Let's not talk about it," I'd find someone else who would listen. Conversely, ignorant of her needs, I'd flood her with too much conversation without giving her time to exercise her need to process information. Invariably, she would shut down, and our relationship would become a stalemate, both parties in a corner afraid to move.

Needs require constant attention! Misunderstood or unfulfilled needs can send your relationship ricocheting back to the superficial levels of intimacy, perhaps even hurtling out the door and toward the heartbreak of divorce. My office is filled with people who, not understanding, much less meeting, their mates' needs, find themselves in deep trouble.

One thing is certain: before you can begin meeting your mate's deepest needs you have to know what they are.

In our marriage conferences around the United States, we passed out a survey called Love: Discovering Your Top Relational Needs—forty-seven questions designed to help us understand people's basic relationship needs. The survey asked the fundamental questions that every person in a serious relationship must answer, or face the consequences of ignorance about perhaps the most important aspect of themselves and their mates.

The Seven Basic Needs: Meet Them or Else!

Needs will take a couple down two divergent paths: fulfilled needs are the great secret of intimate relationships; unmet needs are the most common relationship downfall.

Our survey, which eventually included more than 10,000 couples, led to an interesting conclusion: what most couples consider to be their top needs are the same needs that, unfulfilled, lead to the main causes of arguments described by the leading researchers in the relationship field. What does this mean? When needs are not being met, look out! Your marriage is at stake. Your mate will become overly defensive, argumentative, jealous, belligerent, withdrawn, or degrading of others. When our deepest relational needs are not met, we tend to be more irritated, discouraged, edgy, hypersensitive, and reactionary to "average" events that occur in a typical marriage.

Let me give you an example. One of the top-ranked needs from our survey is to be included when decisions are made affecting the marriage. No one enjoys being controlled by a mate. But a husband who believes his wife is controlling the marriage, who believes his wife is too "bossy," may start an argument over something so minute as his wife's offhanded request to take out the trash, instead of tackling the bigger, more dangerous subject of her domination. The husband might feel that his feelings or wishes are not considered often enough. So he draws a line in the sand over the little matter of taking out the trash, because if he doesn't take a stand somewhere, she will literally steam-roll over him. He's not telling her that he thinks she is too bossy. That would bring on the Big Argument, so he settles for the smaller battle, the trash. She would be confused, of course. Why would he be so upset over taking out the trash? But the real hidden issue is the need for power and control. The real issue is, "Who's the boss in our home?"

Here are the top seven needs identified from our surveys, not ranked in any particular order. I've listed the needs 1–7, but I have devised the list as a short test for you to take, so that you may rank these needs in order of how important they are to both you and your mate. Take the time right now to pick your top three needs and to guess what your mate's will be.

Here are the seven basic needs from our survey:

1. The need to feel connected through (a) talking or (b) spending recreational time together as a couple ____

2. The need to feel accepted and valued for (a) who I am (my opinions, thoughts, and beliefs) and (b) what I do ____

3. The need to feel my mate is being (a) honest and (b) trustworthy ____

4. The need to feel a mutual commitment that we'll stay together and feel secure in love ____

5. The need to feel I'm being included in most decisions that affect (a) my life (because I want to become a "We," not just a "Me," as I was before marriage) or (b) the need to feel I'm being included in most decisions that affect my marriage (Who's the boss?) ____

6. The need to feel that my mate is giving me (a) verbal or (b) physical tenderness ____

7. The need to feel that we are maintaining a mutually vibrant spiritual relationship ____

Our survey showed a major difference between the needs of men and women:

Women's Needs

* I have a need from my husband to . . .

1. Be honest and trustworthy.
2. Honor and value my opinions, thoughts, and beliefs.
3. Know that we'll stay together and feel secure in love.
4. Maintain a mutually vibrant spiritual relationship.
5. Feel accepted, valued, and respected for who I am.
6. Feel connected through talking.
7. Agree on how to raise our children.
8. Be included in most decisions that affect my life or marriage.
9. Resolve differences, conflicts, and arguments.
10. Feel connected by spending time together as a couple.

In our survey, women rated "Feel connected through talking" as a much greater need than men did. Women rated "Feel connected by spending time together as a couple" as a much greater need than men did. Women rated "Be touched nonsexual ways" as a much greater need than men did.

Women rated "Receive verbal tenderness" as a much greater need than men did.

Women rated "Periodically update his knowledge of my greatest needs" as a much greater need than men did. Women rated "Feel safe when I share who I am" as a much greater need than men did. And Women rated "Understand my personality and gender differences" as a much greater need than men did.

Seven Additional Relational Needs for Women

I need my husband to:

1. Connect more with me through talking.
2. Spend time together with me alone.
3. Touch me more in nonsexual ways.
4. Give me verbal tenderness at both normal and tense times.
5. Periodically update his knowledge of my greatest needs as I age and change.
6. Help me feel safe when I share who I am.
7. Understand and value my personality and gender differences.

Men's Needs

I have a need from my wife to . . .

1. Be honest and trustworthy.
2. Know that we'll stay together and feel secure in love.
3. Maintain a mutually vibrant spiritual relationship.
4. Feel accepted, valued, and respected for who I am.
5. Be included in most decisions that affect my life or marriage.
6. Resolve differences, conflicts, and arguments.
7. Feel accepted, valued, and respected for what I do.
8. Honor and value my opinions, thoughts, and beliefs.
9. Agree on how to raise our children.
10. Gain agreement and harmony in decision making.
11. Become emotionally healthy (e.g., resolve personal issues).
12. Resolve her prolonged anger.

In our survey men rated "Have sex" as a much greater need than women did. Men rated "Participate in recreational or fun times together" as a greater need than women did. Men also rated "Spend time at home" as a greater need than women did.

Four Additional Relational Needs of Men

I need my wife to . . .

1. Initiate sex more often.
2. Participate in recreational or fun times together with me.
3. Praise me more often for what she may consider as "little" things I do for her and the family.
4. Help create a pleasant, harmonious atmosphere at home because I'd like being home.

Now, create your own "hierarchy of needs" by ranking them, using the following questions and exercises. Please take the time to check these needs and see if they relate to you or your mate. If so, include them in your hierarchy of needs as well.

1. Which needs are the most important in your life? Rank each of them from 0 to 10. Are there any additional ones important to you? Are any of those needs important to you?

2. Which of your needs are already being met by your mate, and how fulfilled are you feeling today? 0 to 10? Thank your mate for the good job and express that you may always need these needs met. But as you grow and change, the needs may change somewhat in intensity or value.

3. Which top three needs would you most want your mate to concentrate on in the coming year? For example, if your mate had only so much energy to give, what are the top three needs you couldn't live without? Which top one, two, or three needs would you love for your mate to increase his or her attention to over the next year? How are those needs being met now, and where would you like the status to be a year from now? What would be the best ways you can think of to achieve that status?

Of course, all these needs mean different things to different people. It's important for you and your mate to go through the list thoroughly and create a mutual understanding of what these needs mean to you individually. Let your mate determine the best ways to meet his or her needs. Do not try to read your mate's mind! He or she knows his or her needs best! In my last book, *Making Love Last Forever*, I list ten possible ways to keep your love alive. The most important ways are those that let your mate know how valuable he or she is everyday and show it by making him or her a priority over other things in life. Let your mate speak freely and openly about the needs important to him or her. You might get to see an integral piece of your mate's heart.

Recognizing your mate's needs is a critical first step, but the force that has the ability to consistently take you to the deepest levels of intimacy is *recharging* these needs on a daily basis.

Recharging Your Mate's Needs Daily

Imagine a seven-cell battery, each cell wired to one of your mate's top basic needs. Now, consider each of these needs as individual power cells in your mate's relational "battery." When those battery cells are drained by everyday living, working, children, friends, and "just life in general," humans need their relational batteries recharged, just like your car battery needs charging after too much neglect or overuse.

What charges car batteries is electricity. What charges human relational batteries is recognizing and charging your partner's needs—and it takes about twenty minutes a day. I learned the "twenty minute theory" from relationship expert Dr. John Gottman. He discovered through his research that the difference between a couple who divorces and one who stays together but unhappy is ten minutes a day of "turning toward" each other daily. By this, he means that a couple must "turn toward" each other every day through conflict-solving or affirmative interactions.

Gottman found that couples who divorced experienced about ten minutes less per day of turning toward each other than couples who stayed together but were unhappy. Furthermore, he found that couples who stay together and are *happy* "turn toward" each other an additional ten minutes more each day than unhappily married couples. From these discoveries we can surmise that a total of twenty minutes a day of "turning toward each other" in substantial ways can make the difference between divorce and staying together in a satisfying relationship.

Dr. Gottman also discovered that it takes five times as many positive "charges" (affirming, positive experiences and conflict resolutions) compared to negative charges (corrosive or combative exchanges) to maintain a healthy relationship every day. Remember these statistics: five-to-one. Twenty minutes a day. They have the power to take your relationship to a deeper, more satisfying level.

What I want you to do is to envision a "relationship battery" within your mate. I like to help couples discover each other's main relational needs and then nurture those needs—"recharge them"—twenty minutes a day. Gottman found that turning toward your spouse might be something as simple as turning your head toward him or her and making eye contact during an ordinary discussion. It might be as simple as nodding and responding to a comment with "I see" or "Yes, I understand." Turning toward is not staying glued to the TV, which can rob your marriage or family of these small, important gestures. If he or she asks, "How'd your day go?" and you ignore the question or snap a sarcastic comment back, then you're moving away, not moving toward. Turning away can be not looking up from your daily newspaper or responding to your spouse's question by saying "I'm too busy right now." Now, I understand people do get busy, but a moving toward response could be as easy as saying, "I'm busy now, but let's talk about it this afternoon."

Your little responses grow into big positive or negative charges—and these charges collect in your mate's mind like power in a car's battery. To maintain five positive charges to each negative one is going to take time and attention. So start concentrating on your daily twenty minutes recharging time! If you're already at the deepest level of intimacy, these twenty minutes can keep you there. If you're not there yet, these twenty minutes can literally propel your relationship to deeper and more satisfying levels. For example, one of my deepest needs is to share fun activities with my wife on "special dates." To recharge this need, all Norma has to do is walk over to me one day during the week and suggest that we go out for dinner and then to one of the music shows in our town. She knows my need and she charges it! I usually drop whatever I'm doing and get ready for a fun night. It gives me such a warm, fuzzy feeling of contentment anytime we do something fun together. It charges my emotional needs battery every time.

Charging the Seven Basic Needs

The following is an explanation of the seven basic needs from my point of view. This is what the seven top basic needs mean to my wife and to me in our own relationship. You will have to decide what your own top needs are and what they mean to you and your mate. Help each other understand how you feel about your own needs and how your needs can be met in ways that will really work for you.

1. The Need to Feel Connected Through (A) Talking or (B) Spending Recreational Time Together as a Couple

This is, of course, the *big one*, the natural yearning of all human beings, the need for connection. It should be so simple and yet it's one of the most common unfulfilled needs. Why? Because men and women are inherently different in their communications processes and techniques.

As Deborah Tannen outlines in her classic book *That's Not What I Meant!* we all have two basic needs that determine what we say and how we say it. First, we have a need to get close to each other, to have a sense of community or connection, to feel we're not alone in the world. But we also have a need to maintain a certain distance from each other to reserve our unique identities, so others don't impose on or engulf us.

We need others in order to survive, but we also need our independence.

Women, she writes, are better at "meta-messages," hinting around at their meaning without saying exactly how they feel or what they want. Generally, men are more straightforward and like to state the facts. We like to exchange straight information. And so because of these different styles of communication—seeking to fulfill our deep basic need for connection—we stay at odds. Both men and women need connection, but neither knows the same way of finding it. That is why so often the basic need for satisfying communication is thwarted. Because of mishandled communication, the most elementary human need of connection can result in a power struggle. "The belief that sitting down and talking will ensure mutual understanding and solve problems is based on the assumption that we can say what we mean, and what we say will be understood as we mean it," writes Tannen. "This is unlikely to happen if conversational styles differ. . . . As relationships continue, if style differences cause misunderstandings, each new misunderstanding gives added evidence for negative conclusions about the other. She is unreasonable, he is uncooperative, she is inconsiderate, he is selfish, she is pushy, he is anti-social. And each new piece of evidence can be stuffed into an already bulging gunnysack of individually minor complaints."

In a sense, we're back to the fundamental reality of inherent and inevitable differences. Women tend to connect through words, men connect through doing activities together like watching TV, sports, or walks. *But when needs are involved, differences must be confronted and dealt with—or the unmet need will undermine the very foundations of your relationship.* Tannen tells a story of a couple, Dora and Tom, to show the different ways men and women seek connection through communication.

If Dora is feeling comfortable and close to Tom, she settles into a chair after dinner and begins to tell him about a problem she is having at work. She expects him to ask questions to show he's interested; reassure her that he understands and that what she feels is normal; and return the intimacy by telling her a problem of his. Instead, Tom sidetracks her story, cracks jokes about it, questions her interpretation of the problem, and gives her advice about how to solve it and avoid such problems in the future.

Tannen notes that women want more "noises" as proof that their mates are listening—the appropriate "uh huh"— while men want less noise or proof that what they're saying is being received. Men use noises to show they agree, women use them to show they are listening. Men, she adds, like to explain "how things work," and they focus on straightforward topics like sports, business, or weather. Women hear these "facts" as a lecture, not a conversation, Tannen observes. Instead, women like to talk about the events and people they met during that day, and they interpret talking about these apparently insignificant things as showing involvement.

Tannen also says that women often find men's "lectures" condescending, as if the men are trying to tell them, "I'm the teacher, listen to me," and they feel belittled by their husbands' tones. Women, in turn, use wide ranges of voice inflection and tend to dramatize the events of their days, a habit men hate; they don't want to relive events. They like to tell a few facts about the weather and such, but not all the details; most men would find that boring and unnecessary. And if a woman presses a man for details, he might withdraw, feeling as if he were under much too intense scrutiny.

These differences in conversational styles detailed in Tannen's book illustrate basic differences between the genders. Neither men nor women are the "bad guys." Most of us genuinely try to be honest and considerate and to communicate, but we sometimes end up in knots anyway, in spite of our best efforts. This happens because our communication is indirect and underdetermined by nature, and also because of inevitable differences in conversational style. Seeing things go wrong, we look for explanations in personality, intentions, or other psychological motivations.

So look beyond your differences and search for a connection deeper than your engendered habits and tendencies!

Here's how to recharge your mate's need for connection:

1. First, recognize your mutual need for connection, but that your communications styles are different.
2. Step back and notice what's going on. See the styles, read the "meta-messages"—the hidden meanings and issues—within your conversation.
3. Videotape or record one of your entire conversations and watch and listen to it. See if you can see what is going on and, once you recognize problems, concentrate on working through them together.

2. The Need to Feel Accepted and Valued for (A) Who I Am (Value my Opinions, Thoughts, and Beliefs) and (B) What I Do

• **Accept and value who I am.** We all need to be actively valued for our opinions, concerns, expectations, thoughts, and beliefs. As we illustrated in previous chapters, we all have our own unique "colors" and need to be valued and treasured for the uniqueness of that color. We all strive to grow and change and become better persons. But our colors may stay pretty much the same for years. Our identity is integral to our happiness. Our fingerprints are ours and no one else's. Each of us is unique, different, special, a treasure—and most of us do not want to be changed! Recharging this need of individuality is simple, yet so many of us spend our relational lifetimes messing it up.

When we value someone else's opinions, concerns, and expectations, it doesn't mean that we have to agree with them. We may have completely different ideas and beliefs, but we can understand that our mates' are different, but no less important, than our own. We can treasure the person that these opinion, concerns, and expectations are coming from. A prime example of two different beliefs living harmoniously would be the famous Democratic campaign manager and author James Carville and his wife, television personality and Republican

Mary Matalin. They have wildly different ideologies when it comes to politics, but they clearly value each other as human beings.

Respect doesn't mean that our mates have to be just like us. In college, I learned to spurn the concept of "ethnocentricity," the belief that whatever you learned as a child, what your parents and good friends believed, "must be right and good." Ethnocentricity dictates that all other beliefs and ways of doing things are somewhat wrong because they are not what you learned. Ethnocentricity is the essence of dishonor. Thinking that you are somehow superior because your upbringing was the "best" gives you no room to accept that others have different opinions, concerns, and expectations.

To charge someone's need for acceptance and value, you must lay down your preconceptions and accept and value your mate for who he or she is. You must, once again, honor the differences and charge the person with positive feedback for the unique individual he or she represents.

For example, I have two good friends who are married but belong to two completely different religious faiths. Their respective faiths are usually in conflict with one another over different doctrines and worship patterns. But my friends have concentrated on finding the similarities between their faiths instead. They focus on what they have in common and how they both love God and cherish their children in God's love. It is always amazing to me that my friends can strive to find the things that they admire about each other's faith and avoid the areas that divide them. They find it possible mainly through practicing the skill of honoring one another.

• **Accept and value what I do.** We must all feel accepted and valued for what we do. This includes work, activities, hobbies, ministries, and services to others. When we find our mates, we become a "we," a couple with them, but it's important to maintain our individuality, our "I" in what we do, especially what we do for a living. Charging this need is also fairly simple. Concentrate on not dominating your mate with your activities or work, but instead allowing your mate to have his or her individual pursuits and dreams. Don't allow your own work or "things" to push aside or overshadow your mate's needs. You can both blossom in the same garden, both separately and together. You become a team.

My wife, Norma, hardly ever cries, but recently, I made an off-handed comment in a business meeting whose members included a business consultant, Norma, and myself. I said something about her "resistance to growth" in our company, and Norma teared up. She then proceeded to offer me a compassionate response to my lack of understanding of what her real heart truly feels regarding our company. All the men in the room—including me—froze and stared at Norma, wondering just where her response would lead. I learned that my honor and respect is one of my wife's major needs. It is very important to her that she knows I understand her unique contributions to our company.

What I realized in this situation is how easy it is to say something off-handed to the person you believe will never leave you and who loves you the most in the world. It's easy to think that you can say most anything to your mate and not think about the consequences or the impact of your words. I have now recommitted myself to being even more careful about what I say about her work. Dr. Gary Oliver recently said to me, "When your mate reacts negatively toward you for something you say or do, remember that it's a treasure in disguise—through the hurt, you can find the relationship need which is being revealed through your mate's reaction to your words and actions."

3. The Need to Feel My Mate is Being Honest and Trustworthy

This need ranked near the top for all of the couples in our needs survey. Why? Because it's the essence of all intimacy: trust and integrity. Does your mate tell the truth most of the time? Can you depend upon him or her? Being honest seems to be part of security. Can you say, "We stay together because he or she is trustworthy and I can count on him or her to be honest with me?"

What happens when we're not honest with our mates?

Don't kid yourself! They always seem to find out. I have a friend who started stealing small amounts of money from his employer. He thought no one would ever know. He was caught by a fellow employee and almost lost his job. I spoke to him about it, and he told me that his lying began to alter him, ever so subtly. He noticed that he was lying about other things more easily. He was more distant in relationships, he was more depressed and defensive. He seemed to be hypersensitive and would snap at his mate over minor things. He felt tired and then realized how much energy it was taking to cover up what he was doing and the subsequent lies that multiplied. It took his wife almost a year to start trusting him again after she discovered what he had done. Lying is like allowing water to slowly seep under a wooden floor. Rot and mildew begin building up and before long, you step on the floor and you fall through the rot. The floor might still look OK to the eye, but rotten floors are very dangerous. It's not hard to spot a rotting marriage . . . trust is the first thing to go.

Honesty and trust are my wife's paramount needs. Once you discover your mate's top needs, it's up to you to learn everything you can about them. All it takes is a question: "What does this need mean to you?" It took me years to ask my wife this question, but once I did, she answered succinctly. "It means following rules and honestly doing the things we know we should do."

In one sentence, Norma showed me miles of the relationship roadmap in her heart. She's not merely concerned about rules, she's fanatical about them. This single need drove most of her actions. Sometimes, I feel like I'm living with an independent prosecutor. On a scale of from 1 to 10, she is about a 9 on keeping the rules. I'm somewhere around a 6 on the need to do everything by the book. It's not that I want to break rules, it's just that I don't have the same drive to keep them all. I see myself as more relaxed and can miss the "perfect" mark now and then.

So we became a couple with battling needs: my need to bend the rules versus her need to obey each and every one. Our little war of needs played out in parking lots ("Why can't I park for two seconds in the 'No Parking' zone?"), grocery stores ("But there's nobody waiting in the express line and we only have five items over the limit!"), and our home (Monopoly and other board games were definitely out!).

Recharging my wife's primary need for honesty was simple. Since I know that this is such a major need, I have made a conscious decision to "give" on points of disagreement involving rules. She has since relaxed and is much more tolerant now of "minor" violations. I spend as much of my minimum twenty minutes a day of "recharging time" by paying more attention to details, especially the rules of life.

4. The Need to Feel a Mutual Commitment that We'll Stay Together and Feel Secure in Love

This is the need for commitment. Relationship expert Dr. Scott Stanley's definition of commitment is twofold. First, he says, commitment involves constraints. Constraints are those forces that keep you and your mate together: kids, in-laws, money, friends, value systems, faith, even the threat of a divorce. But the constraint aspect of commitment is not strong enough to keep couples together and happily married forever. For that, Stanley says, a couple must also have dedication. Couples with dedication not only plan to stay together, they have a constantly evolving *plan* to stay together. They rededicate themselves to each other regularly through planning events and talking about the future.

If you're interested in discovering more on this important topic, read Dr. Stanley's book on this, *The Heart of Commitment*. For now, here's a guideline for you to recharge your mate's need for a lifetime together, a way for you to implement your dedication and show your commitment to your relationship:

• *Plan several activities and dreams you'll be doing together over the next twenty years.* Where do you want to travel? What goals do you both have together and separately that your mate can help you accomplish? What do you want to do together

224 • GARY SMALLEY

with your children? What projects do you desire to finish? Any future educational paths that might be mutually enriching? How about buying a boat big enough to live on for a while? My wife and I sat down recently and made a plan to follow our dreams of taking two major trips per year. We decided that one of the trips would be with our three grown children and grand-kids; the other will be reserved exclusively for the two of us. We took our first one last year: Norma's dream trip to England and Ireland. It was her dream because I gave her a major charge: she was responsible for planning each day of the trip. Then, an amazing thing happened. I thought I was charging Norma's needs, but I ended up getting charged myself. It became my fa-vorite vacation, because every day, Norma would insist that I find a place to fish on our way to something that she wanted to see or do. It worked out so well that we're trying it again.

• *Write out an agreement on what you plan to do for the next twenty years to keep your love alive.* Here's a contract for you to consider for lasting love:

We agree to enter the fourth and fifth levels of intimacy whenever the other one so desires. We will do this by deeply listening to each other, not defending our own opinions, but striving to love, understand, and validate the other's feelings and needs.

We agree to highly value each other and consider each other as more important than anything else on earth, except possibly our relationship with God. If gold could describe our honor for each other, we would each be married to a 24-carat person.

We agree to communicate with each other regularly. This will be accomplished by speaking to each other by shar-ing truthful loving information and listening carefully to un-derstand and validate each other's uniqueness. Our preferred method of communication will be drive-through listening. Our everyday conversations will include the safety necessary to share opinions, concerns, and expectations.

We agree never to go to sleep at night without resolving our major differences or conflicts. We will forgive each other as needed.

We agree to find creative ways of meeting each other's deepest relational needs. As we each grow older and change, we will strive to stay current with our understanding of each other's needs and ways of meeting those needs.

Now, back to our guideline for recharging your mate's needs:

• *Express your lifetime commitment in words.* Print it on a plaque, say it with gifts, just plain say it. "I will be with you forever and keep loving you until death do us part." Write a poem and print it for the whole family to see.

• *Become a student of your mate.* Find out all you can about who she or he is. What are your mate's favorite foods, activities, clothes, dreams? Take the color test and treasure your mate's special differences.

• *When conflict arises.* Employ the three skills that can take you to the deepest level of intimacy. Write down how you plan to implement each of these skills in your relationship. Remember, the three skills: (1) Keep honor alive daily; (2) use drive-through listening after you have a serious argument and have given yourselves time to calm down; and (3) lovingly recharge your mate twenty minutes per day in the areas in which your mate needs your care.

Another type of commitment that couples need from one another is a willingness to keep searching for solutions to problems between them. Thousands of couples have expressed the need to feel that each has a working plan to resolve personal problems or conflicts. After thirty-five years of marriage, my wife and I have discovered that we feel secure and included in all aspects of our relationship because of the establishment of a simple plan for solving disagreements. Here are our steps:

• We first try to resolve the disagreement by simply discussing the situation as calmly as we can. We go back and forth trying to understand each other's positions. We can do this on most subjects. Either she or I will see a logical solution or compromise that we can settle on. In this way we have truly become one, a successful "blending of two individuals to-gether." Occasionally, we hit the wall of anger on some subject and start defending our positions with enthusiasm. That can lead to escalation of anger, so we usually take a time out and wait until we both calm down and take the next step.

• We head to a restaurant. Yes, that's right. We calmly sit down at the table or at a restaurant. We can't go out of control with other people there. We use drive-through listening and argue by the rules. We hold an object—a fork, spoon, or can-dle—when we are sharing our feelings or needs about the situ-ation. The one not holding the object simply paraphrases what is being said to gain as much understanding as possible. We take turns passing the object back and forth until we both feel completely understood and validated. Then we start sharing any ideas we can think of that would solve the situation in a win-win way. We use our creative juices to think of some solu-tion to fit both of our feelings and needs. It almost always works. But sometimes we can't do it on our own, so we move to the next step.

• We ask two or three of our trusted friends to sit with us as we use drive-through listening again. This step has never failed to work. We always go away from the meeting with friends with a solution we can both live with, and it feels really safe to know we can always solve our disagreements. Our friends are like the grand jury—they just help us say what our feelings are and what we need out of the solution. There have been times when Norma and I have been upset with each other during the group meeting, but it has always ended in peace. If it didn't, we would develop the next step. We haven't had to move to another step, so I can't tell you what it is yet. But if we were forced into it, we'd keep trying different actions until we found the method that worked best for us. We keep trying, we never give up—which is, of course, another instance of a positive charge, a way to say, "You're so central in my life I'll do anything to get through problems and clear the way to deeper intimacy."

5. The Need to Feel I'm Being Included in Most Decisions that Affect (A) My Life or (B) My Marriage

Power and control. These are the forces that undermine many a marriage. If you're constantly asking yourself, "Who's the boss?" you likely are suffering from power and control issues. It's unhealthy to acquire extreme attitudes, whether yours is too detached ("Do whatever you want, I don't care.") or too domineering ("You'll do whatever I say and like it."). Democracy is still the best system. Finding a win-win solution is the ideal scenario—and the best way to charge your mate's need for equality. Both mates feel valued and cared for when they like the solution to a conflict. It's normal for couples to disagree about many things: raising the children, money, in-laws, leisure time, sex. The list is endless because you and your mate are so different in gender and background.

But there is a way out of the power and control trap! It's called honoring and loving each other. When you love someone, you care about every part of that person, especially his or her needs and dreams. Every time my wife and I have a major decision before us, we refer to a process, a "decision chart." First, we write the issue we're discussing across the top of a page. Then, we list all of the reasons, pro and con, for and against moving ahead on the matter. Third, we evaluate each reason. We ask questions: What will the effects be of this decision? Will it propel our relationship to deeper or shallower levels of intimacy? Is it selfish or will it help others? Finally, we total the pros and cons and the winning resolution—to move forward or to decide against—wins the debate.

This process is a major charge for both of our needs for equality. Snap decisions, which always seem to favor one party more than the other, are no longer part of the equation. The facts are presented, debated, then tallied. Try it next time you have a major decision to make. You'll be surprised at how easy—and empowering—decision making can become.

6. The Need to Feel that My Mate Is Giving Me (A) Verbal or (B) Physical Tenderness

Now, we're talking about affection, something no intimate relationship can do without. However, affection, like most needs,
means different things to different people. In his book *His
Needs, Her Needs,* author Willard Harley Jr. creates the following hierarchy of men's and women's needs.

WOMEN	MEN
Affection	Sexual fulfillment
Conversation	Relational companionship
Honesty and openness	An attractive spouse
Financial support	Domestic support
Family commitment	Admiration

The difference is enlightening. A woman's top need is for
affection, while a man's top need is for sexual fulfillment. The
need for physical tenderness is unequivocal to both genders,
but they go about getting it different ways. In his book, Harley
tells a story about a wife who, after being denied real affection
from her husband, was literally swept into an affair with a co-
worker who simply hugged her regularly. "What happened?"
writes Harley. "Did Jane's wedding vows mean nothing to her?
Was she just waiting for the chance to two-time her husband?
Hardly. Jane simply felt so starved for affection that she was
literally hugged into having an affair!"

If you're a man, remember that affection is to a woman
what water is to a plant: without it, she will literally shut
down. Hug her and kiss her every time you enter and leave
your home. Phone her whenever you're apart. Tell her how
much she means to you. Bring flowers, candy, gifts, cards.
Never forget her birthday and, especially, your anniversary.
Plan surprises. Help her with the housework. Never let the
night fall without telling her you love her. And always remember: affection does not mean sex.

Don't worry if it isn't in your basic nature to be tender. It's certainly not in mine. There are times when things happen in our house and Norma feels low or tired. Combine that with low blood sugar levels and off to the races we can go, galloping straight into an argument. But I have noticed in the past few years that if I can just hold her and listen to her tenderly, she is quickly energized again, and the next day she will thank me for being so understanding. All I have to do is just listen and remain gentle without trying to "solve" anything. At first, this seemed like a waste of time to me, but through the years, I have seen the great value of being tender toward her just because it fulfills such a deep need in her.

If you're a woman, remember: his need for affection is as strong as yours, although he may express it differently. Follow the guidelines I've written for men—charge, charge, and recharge your mate's bottomless battery with verbal and physical tenderness.

7. The Need to Feel that We Are Maintaining a Mutually Vibrant Spiritual Relationship

Religion and other core belief systems are bound to play a part in your relationship, since, as Markman, Stanley, and Blumberg note in *Fighting for Your Marriage*, research has shown that religious people are the most likely to get married to begin with. They report that Fran Dickson of the University of Denver discovered that couples who have stayed together for fifty years have a "shared relationship vision"—that is, these couples have created a common perspective including personal dreams and goals for the future that helps them support a long-term view of commitment to each other and their lives together. Markman, Stanley, and Blumberg suggest that a shared belief system—"including mutual understanding about the meaning of life, death, and marriage"—can help nurture this relationship vision.

You can also nurture your relationship vision by tending to your spiritual relationship with your mate. Whether your beliefs are similar or on opposite ends of the spectrum, if you respect, validate, and nurture your mate's beliefs, you will strengthen your bond. Whatever your belief system, it is no doubt a part of your daily life, intrinsic to your identity. You and your mate must remember to recharge this part of your life regularly.

Giving Your Mate Daily Charges

How do you recharge your mate's relational batteries? There's the *direct charge* and the *indirect charge,* also known as the repair method. We've just finished reviewing the seven topranked basic needs. Now, let's look closer at two methods of charging your mate's relational battery by fulfilling his or her basic needs.

The Direct Charge

This is the simplest, most straightforward way of charging your mate's battery. Here's a step-by-step guide.

• Loving communication always charges needs. The deeper and more meaningful your communication, the stronger the charge. Sometimes people just say what's on the top of their head and don't really understand it until they hear it paraphrased back to them through drive-through listening and/or using emotional word pictures. These communication techniques are among the best ways you can charge your mate's needs daily. The skills illustrate the essence of listening, understanding, and validating. (Review Chapter 6 if you need refreshment on this powerful system of communication.) Remember that emotional word pictures are where you phrase your feelings and needs within some type of linguistic "picture" or story that your mate can "see or feel." Here's an example: "I feel like this flower right here. See, it's drooping and needs water." Word pictures allow you to take 100 percent responsibility for your own emotions and needs.

• Use humor in an honoring way. It's another direct deposit, especially when you encounter conflict or tension. Whenever possible, be light, carefree, and funny—make your mate laugh. Use drive-through listening in a humorous way to reduce tension. Here's an example. You've just spilled orange juice over the new carpet and your mate is fuming. Using the drive-through listening method you say, "Let me say what I think you're saying. You think I spilled the juice on the carpet on purpose just to ruin your day." Say it with a grin. It's better than reacting negatively and allowing a full-blown argument—and the negative charges that go with it—to ensue. Laughter is not only contagious; it carries a positive charge!

• Remind yourself every day and tell your family how valuable your mate is. If your mate is not the most valuable person in your life, then make a conscious decision to increase his or her value in your heart. Raise that value to the highest level. Simply tell your mate, "I love you. You are very valuable to me." Look him or her right in the eyes, and speak slowly and gently. The first three to thirty seconds of any conversation determines the next two hours of conversation. If you start out harshly, you will likely endure two hours of harshness. If you start soft and gentle and loving, you will have two hours of soft, gentle, and loving conversation. It's a major charge.

• Soften your words, especially if you are bringing up something that may get a reaction from your mate. Use gentle and honoring voice inflections. Take full responsibility for all of your emotions and needs. Don't blame your mate or family for how you feel. You are choosing whatever set of emotions you have by the thinking patterns and choices you've made up to the present time. Feelings always follow actions, choices, and thinking.

• Touch your loved ones. Practice the words of the great James Taylor song: "Shower the people you love with love, tell them the way that you feel. . . ." Reach out to your mate regularly with a gentle touch. Ask your mate how many times he or she needs to be touched every day in order to maintain emotional strength. Then, follow that advice.

• Plan fun times in the future. Just plan, even if you don't end up doing anything! Women have told me that they find more joy in the planning of something than in actually doing it. That doesn't mean you shouldn't make good on your plans, but remember that the fun and the charge is in the planning itself.

• Step out of your ordinary role. If you're a businessman, try surprising your wife by cleaning the house. Believe it or not, house cleaning is a major positive charge. Guess what the number one answer was in a nationwide poll about what turns a woman on sexually? More than anything else, women said they get turned on when their husbands clean the house. Reminiscing is another major positive charge. Improving yourself by reading a book charges your mate. Improving yourself by going to counseling or to a seminar also sends a charge. Step out of your ordinary role!

• Maintain a carefree spirit. Play games, talk about your children, discuss fun topics, and give gifts. Give gifts regularly! It's a major charge. If you can't give a material gift, give a physical one. Just an encouraging nod is a charge. Forgiveness is even better. Share the enjoyable events of the past week. Discuss fun topics. Talk about your mutual friends or your children. Play games.

In summary, stay as calm as possible, keep your heart rate down, and use as many of the above methods to "charge" your relationship for a minimum twenty minutes each and every day. Encourage your mate to voice his or her needs to you, the needs that really need charging, and do the same for them. Then, charge, charge, and recharge your mate's basic needs.

The Repair or Redirect Charge

The second method of emotional needs-charging works sort of like an automobile's braking system. You can use this charge whenever you recognize that you are heading in a negative direction in your relationship. If you and your mate start arguing or attacking each other verbally, stop! Literally stop your actions, your conversation, your processes. Stop, look, and listen to what you and your mate are saying.

Here are a few methods to use the repair or redirect charge:

• *Request time-out.* Just call a temporary truce to calm down or consider how you might discuss the matter through drive-through listening. Your mate will get a definite charge from your willingness to stop and analyze the situation before plowing full-steam ahead into an argument. Your ability to take a time-out marks an important decision: you are showing that you do not want to let yourself or your emotions get out of control. For years in my own marriage, I allowed myself and our arguments to spiral in negative directions. I would start lecturing Norma. But we don't let that happen anymore. We employ the indirect charge, the braking system, every time we realize we're heading in a negative direction in a discussion. Try it next time you find yourself in similar straits. Simply stop and say, "This is not worth it." Keep your heart rate down. Smile. Or simply change the subject. You can also use humor or drive-through listening, or a combination of both.

• *Consider changing the subject.* You'll discover that even the most heated arguments have a small substance at their core, even though the small substance is most likely tied to a major unfulfilled need. Offering to move on by changing the subject—especially if you're the one expressing a problem—charges your mate by showing him or her that you value the relationship over the issue at hand.

• *Acknowledge fault.* Confessing that your actions or words may have turned the marriage in a negative direction is a major charge. Admit hurtful behavior as soon as possible and seek forgiveness. Remember this rule: the one being hurt must acknowledge the hurt. So when you say, "I was wrong to say that, could you forgive me?" make sure your mate acknowledges the hurt and realizes your plea for forgiveness. Once you admit fault, don't dwell on it. Show immediate empathy by saying something like, "This must be very upsetting to you, more than I can understand." Take a short time to figure out the situation before saying anything else. Assure each other that you'll return and discuss the matter in a positive way. (Drive-through listening is a good method to employ when you do return to the subject.)

• *Ban disagreements during "special" times.* Remember that you're in this relationship together. Nobody wants a vacation, date, drive, or Sunday afternoon ruined. So create a law in your love life: no disagreements on special days. If they arise, agree to shelve them until another time.

• *Use the "sandwich method."* This is where you add words of praise before mentioning anything else that may be perceived as negative. Then end the conversation with more words of praise, literally sandwiching the possible negatives within words of praise. Here's an example:

POSITIVE: *"Honey, I know how hard you work for this family and we all deeply appreciate what you do."*
NEGATIVE: *"So when you were late getting home last night from work, I was frustrated only because I was expecting a call from you."*
POSITIVE: *"You are very responsible, and I just appreciate it when you have called in the past."*

• *Show empathy.* Understanding language like, "I can see that you are hurting now," and "I didn't realize that what I said would upset you so much," are better than the empty silence of letting your words fester. Say something that acknowledges that you value your mate and are trying to understand how he or she is feeling.

• *Employ the "transitioning" conversational style.* This is where you acknowledge your mate's comments, but redirect their comments in a more positive, sometimes even humorous, direction. An example:

"Hon, I can see that my being late is upsetting to you. So I'm going in to work tomorrow and fire my boss. Honestly, before this week is out, I'll present you with a well-thought out plan to try and solve this upsetting situation."

The key is "transitioning" from a negative direction by talking about something that charges both of you. Transition into happy memories you've shared, stories about your family and friends, anything that is pleasant and fun. Suggest that you take a break from the negative issues at hand by playing one of your favorite games or taking a walk or a drive.

• "Edit" your words before speaking. Ask yourself, "Is what I'm about to say going to be hurtful to my mate?" If so, edit out the negative! You can also use "editing" for words you've already said. Just say, "I'm sorry for what I've just said. Will you please forgive me?" Or, "Let me phrase this in a different way, because I believe I was misunderstood."

As you can see, analyzing and adjusting just a few aspects of the way you speak to your mate has the potential to revolutionize your relationship. You can empower your interaction with your mate by charging your communication—directly or indirectly. Believe me, the effort you put into making your communication more positive will come back to you exponentially.

The Power of Twenty Minutes

By now, you may have discovered your mate's basic needs, how they stack up for you individually, and how to charge them at least twenty minutes daily. So get started! You can begin as simply as this: since you and your mate know twenty minutes is the minimum time needed for daily charging, set aside twenty minutes each day—before or after dinner, in the morning twenty minutes before the alarm clock's buzz, during lunches—and consciously begin the recharging process.

Start with the list of both you and your mate's basic needs. Then, write out activities beside each need that would charge it. Do this work in a place where you're both comfortable. Eliminate feelings of guilt or selfishness; after all,

236 • GARY SMALLEY

you're recharging each other and you'll soon discover that the more you concentrate on your mate's needs, the more you will be able to meet some of your own needs in the process. Employ drive-through listening for needs maintenance. Build holidays or anniversaries or vacations around specific needs.

Finally, use this list to create "positive charges" and avoid "negative drains."

Positive Charges	Negative Drains
Praise, agreeing with a good idea verbally	Criticism (attacking mate's actions)
Affection	Contempt (condescending or belittling mate)
Understanding, listening	Defending your opinion
Open and honest expression	Emotional or verbal withdrawal
Connection and involvement	Isolation
Cooperation, drive-through listening	Seeking too much control or power
Acceptance, tolerance	Disapproval of mate's uniqueness
Fun, humor	Bad moods, sulking
Honor, speaking well of mate	Disgracing or degrading mate
Showing positive interest	Disinterest
Verbal tenderness	Harshness
Caring	Neglecting joy or sadness
Forgiving spirit	Vindictive attitude
Validation	Invalidation
Empathetic	Falsely interpreting motives or feelings

Once you begin scheduling your twenty minutes a day, I think you'll be surprised at the power it will inject into your relationship. You will not only have arrived at the deepest level of intimacy, you'll have discovered a way to stay there.

CHAPTER EIGHT

A New Beginning

"Marriage is a school of exercise and virtue."
—*Jeremy Taylor, sermon, 1651*

NOW THAT YOU'VE reached the end of this book, your real journey is just beginning: the day-by-day maintenance of your relationship. Your arrival at this important juncture deserves a celebration. So forget your surroundings for a moment and imagine yourself at a wedding. The air is heady with the scent of flowers and the sound of music, the congregation anxiously awaiting the lucky couple's traditional march down the aisle. The music swells, building to a stirring crescendo, announcing the arrival of the bride. Heads turn, necks crane to catch sight of her as she floats down the aisle. She's an angel dressed in a cloud of white, walking toward her destiny, her groom, who stands as if awaiting a dream, a gift from above.

But you're not watching the procession from the congregation. This time, it's you at the altar. That's right. You have been given the opportunity of a lifetime, the chance for a new beginning, to revolutionize your relationship using the techniques and three main skills of optimum relationships revealed in this book. Equipped with this knowledge, you're ready and eager to take your relationship from the slippery shoals of superficiality through the five levels of intimacy, to the deepest depths of love.

The preacher stands before you beaming with a secret that you're about to discover big time in front of your friends and family. Amid the deepening silence, he begins the marriage ceremony—not the time-worn vows, verses, poems, and recitations so frequently voiced once and then forgotten, but a test, perhaps the most important test you'll ever take in your life.

Unless you can prove to him—*right now at this altar!*—that you understand and are willing to live by the tenets of optimum relationships, then the wedding is off and you and your mate will have to return to square one in your education. Unless you can prove yourself worthy of the opportunity you have been presented—a chance at true and lasting love—your vows will go unspoken, your cake will go uncut, and your guests will be sent home to await announcement that you are ready—truly ready—to begin the journey of your lifetime. You are literally fighting for your marriage before it has even begun; you have to prove yourself worthy of this transcendent moment.

The preacher extends his arms and begins: "You stand here this day with a rare and exciting knowledge: a special confidence that your marriage is not only going to last, but your love is going to endure," he says and the congregation hushes into silence.

> Unlike today's flowers, which will wilt, and today's music, which will fade, and today's congregation, which will disperse, the marriage that we are here to celebrate stands a chance of enduring, even thriving, because you have learned a set of all-important techniques and skills. Relationships require daily attention. Therefore, before you say "I do," I want to ensure that you know not only know how to drive your relationship but also exactly where you are going. Every fully realized relationship is a descent from surface emotions to the depths of love and intimacy. It's not a journey of distance—years alone do not make a marriage—but instead a journey of *depth*. You are embarking upon that journey now, that descent to the deepest end of the emotional ocean.

He stares at you and your mate.

"Are you ready to begin the descent?" he asks.

"We are," you say in unison. And the preacher, pleased, knowingly nods his head and addresses the congregation.

I know they this couple is ready because we met last week and I heard for myself what they have learned and what they plan to do from this day forward to make their marriage thrive. But, as I told them in our meeting, I will not marry them until they stand upon this altar and prove their relationship knowledge, especially the three basic skills that will propel them toward intimacy, to you as a congregation, while reaffirming these tenants to themselves.

He turns once again to you and your future spouse.

"Can you prove to all of us that you're ready to begin the journey?" he asks.

And you respond by saying that you are not merely ready, you're eager to begin. You're now well versed in the skills, techniques, and recent theories of optimum relationships, proving that the once-foreboding secrets of love have become a predictable science, as simple, and yet as enlightening, as the discovery by the eighteenth-century surgeons who realized that postoperative infection was killing patients because they were using unsterilized instruments. You realize that equally profound insights are available today regarding "infected" marriages and you now know the skills to avoid the divorce epidemic infecting our world and are equipped with the tools to prevent the relational pitfalls that can take you straight from this sunny altar into the shadow lands of heartbreak. You're confident that you will avoid these dangers. By reaching the end of this book, you're able to prove to the preacher, your mate, and yourself that you know the tenets of optimum relationships.

You realize that a relationship is not a static experience but an active journey through five levels of intimacy, which you and your mate now review with the preacher, the congregation, and yourselves.

• **The first level of intimacy: speaking in clichés.** Here there is no discussion about life or each other; everything will be "fine" and "nice" and "no problem," until one day you awaken and discover that your relationship has been as empty as your conversation.

• **The second level of intimacy: sharing facts.** The fact-sharing stage is the language of incontestable statements—statements about work, the evening news, the children's activities, the weather—used to avoid any chance of conflict.

• **The third level of intimacy: sharing opinions.** Once you begin to share your opinions, concerns, and expectations, you both are at greater risk for starting an argument. Opinions are the ground where battles break out, but there are skills that can overcome differences. If you have not learned how to handle arguments at this level, you are at risk for developing one or all of the four divorce factors.

• **The fourth level of intimacy: sharing feelings.** The fourth level is achieved when both partners feel safe to share their deepest feelings. You have learned both to listen and to voice your opinions, concerns, and expectations to each other without fear of invalidation. There is an underlying atmosphere of honor—that is, the listener tries to understand and validate what is communicated by the speaker. When we share our feelings, we fulfill our deepest relational need. Conflicts reveal that a person's feelings and needs are not being understood, validated, or fulfilled.

• **The fifth level of intimacy: sharing needs.** Level five is different from previous levels, this is where you feel safe to share your own deepest needs. You feel safe, secure, and intimate with each other.

But you not only understand the roadmap, you also know the destination: the fourth and fifth levels of intimacy, the most satisfying and enriching part of marriage. You realize the danger of stalling at the superficial levels, especially the third level—sharing opinions—which is the "woe zone" where an estimated 50 percent of American couples are prisoners behind the wall of conflict. Of those stuck at the third level, only 50 percent remain married; of those, only 25 percent maintain satisfying relationships.

You do not have to be prisoned behind the wall. You know that intimacy begins with communication, the vessel by which human beings descend to the deepest levels. It takes the average individual six years to reach the deepest levels of intimacy—the levels of sharing feelings and needs—but the average marriage lasts only five and a half years. Therefore, you haven't a second to waste! You are equipped and ready to begin the journey immediately, nurturing your relational intelligence just as you can nurture your educational intelligence in school.

You and your partner have dedicated yourselves to assessing where you are in your communication process, the depth meter in your journey to intimacy. If you find yourselves in the shallowest level, speaking in clichés, you will promise not to remain there long. You'll recognize the cliché style of conversation for what it is, an insidious cycle of repetition and banality. You will marshal your energies and employ a three-part technique to break the cliché cycle, confronting the cliché head-on, challenging the unspoken cliché, and turning clichés into facts. You'll use "pattern interrupts"—unexpected, frequently humorous language and actions to deter your mate from resorting to clichés—and ask leading questions, the retail sales technique designed to force your mate into more meaningful conversation.

Once you move on to the next level of intimacy—sharing facts—you'll strive to move beyond it with equally rapid speed. You'll recognize the three species of facts: facts as words, facts as actions, and facts as silence. You'll break the chain of speaking in facts by steering your mate toward the next level of intimacy—sharing opinions—celebrating every time you share an opinion, instead of contesting, attacking, or belittling your mate.

Next comes the hard part, successfully moving through the most dangerous stage of intimacy—sharing opinions—which involves traveling through the mine field of conflict. This is where so many couples forget where they're headed, succumb to the temptation of conflict, and begin the madden-ing dance of conflict, whose steps go something like this:

• *Critical remarks.* Every time you progress to sharing opinions, concerns, and expectations—whenever you get "real" with each other—you can hit what feels like a wall, and that's exactly what it is: the wall of conflict. Unable to reconcile your differences, one or both partner berates the other: "Look what you did!" "Why are you so impractical?" "Look how much you spent!" The journey toward intimacy comes to a screeching halt and the verbal jousting begins.

• *Condescending comments.* Bam, bam, bam! The words land like blows. "Why can't you ever do anything right?" "Why can't you ever be on time?" "You're just like your mother/father/sister/brother!" Couples make cutting comments to pro-tect individual emotional turfs instead of working together for the good of the relationship.

• *Return to safer levels.* Because conflict is painful, one partner—or both—retreats from conflict, returning to the safer levels of superficiality, speaking in clichés, and sharing facts. In these shallow levels a couple can languish for days, months, years, or decades before they again share opinions and the three steps of the dance begin anew: criticism, condescension, and a return to safer levels.

You know where this dance can take you: to the four main divorce patterns—withdrawing from an argument, escalating an argument, invalidating each other during an argument, and having exaggerated or false beliefs about a mate during an ar-gument. All four factors occur at the third level of intimacy—the level of sharing opinions—and they block couples from reaching the deeper levels.

The secret to avoiding the dance? Having the courage to look beyond your own selfish emotions and attitudes to see and utilize conflict for what it is: an inevitable aspect of every relationship that, if properly faced instead of ignored, can de-liver you to the deepest levels of intimacy. You have learned to recognize conflict as a door, an opportunity to be embraced, instead of a confrontation to be avoided. You will no longer

244 • GARY SMALLEY

react to conflict with fear, avoidance, anger, or frustration by attacking your mate instead of the deeper problem. Most of all, you will have learned to honor your differences. It was, after all, your differences that first attracted you and your mate to each other. You were seeking "completion," not separateness, and your differences are the pieces that can make your psychological puzzle complete.

When conflict arises, you can work through it by employing your arsenal of three basic skills of optimum relationships—honor, communication, and recharging your mate's "needs battery" through love. These skills can deliver you to the deepest and most satisfying levels of intimacy.

Standing at this marriage altar, you've proclaimed the first skill—honor—as your top priority. You know the definition of honor: the decision to place high value, worth, and importance on someone, viewing him or her as a priceless gift and considering that person worthy of great respect. You have decided to give your mate the distinction of honor, whether or not the person likes it, wants it, or deserves it.

You realize that honor involves deciding that your mate's opinions, concerns, and expectations are just a little more valuable than your own. In other words, you choose to be a LUVR. When opinions, concerns, and expectations are involved in your conversation with your mate, you will *L*isten, *U*nderstand, *V*alue, and *R*espond with win-win solutions.

You realize that honoring the similarities between you and your mate will be easy, but true honor is the act of recognizing, respecting, and accepting your mate's differences. Once you make the decision to honor your differences with your mate, you will have the courage to walk through the door that will be opened for you, revealing a place where you can fully discover the heart and soul of your mate. You pledge to practice honor on a daily basis by saying it, writing it, posting it, and proclaiming it. You will especially honor this day, your wedding day, as a sacred touchstone of your everlasting honor for each other and return to it daily in your heart, mind, and spirit.

Next, you demonstrate your knowledge of the second skill of optimum relationships: successful and meaningful communication, beginning with *listening,* not searching for solutions. You realize that every human being has a fundamental and essential need to be heard in order to grow and thrive, and you recognize drive-through listening as a powerful communication method that allows each mate to be a LUVR. When your mate feels listened to, understood, and validated, then as a team you can construct a win-win solution to any argument.

You are now well versed in the techniques of drive-through listening: one mate states his or her feelings and needs while the second mate listens and paraphrases those statements until both understand each other completely and can create a win-win solution. You've promised to take the "clerk" role first and to listen carefully in order to totally understand and value what your mate is trying to say. You realize that two mates struggling over the same role—customer or clerk—is not a way to solve an argument. This act of listening to understand each other is called "blending," and it combines two individual viewpoints into a unity. You realize you're no longer two individuals, but two people constantly melding together in your love, always respecting and valuing the uniqueness of the other.

Finally, you practice the third skill of optimum relationships: recharging your mate's "needs battery" through love. You recognize that the conflicts that will threaten your relationship arise from unfulfilled needs. You have taken the words of author Stephen Covey to heart: every major conflict between couples is the result of someone's needs not being met. Realizing that men and women have inherently different needs and different means by which to have these needs fulfilled, you pledge to discover your mate's most important needs and work diligently to meet those needs every day. You have identified and ranked the basic needs of you and your mate, beginning with the main needs identified in this book: (1) the need to feel connected through talking or spending recreational time together as a couple; (2) the need to feel accepted and valued for who you are and what you do; (3) the need to feel that your mate is being honest and trustworthy; (4) the need to feel a mutual commitment that you and your mate will stay together and feel secure in love; (5) the need to feel you are being included in most decisions that affect your life and marriage; (6) the need for verbal or physical tenderness; and (7) the need to feel that you are both maintaining a mutually vibrant spiritual relationship.

You know these needs are wired into your mate's psyche like a seven-cell battery wired to his or her basic needs. You know how to recharge these cells when they are drained by everyday living, and you have promised these recharges for at least twenty minutes each day. You remember relationship expert Dr. John Gottman's discovery that twenty minutes a day of turning toward each other in substantial ways makes the difference between divorce and staying together in a satisfying relationship. When you and your mate encounter conflict or tension, you know you can use indirect charges such as editing your language, softening your voice, or employing the techniques of word pictures or drive-through listening to fulfill your mate's needs for healthy conflict resolution.

You know there's more—much more—involved in making a marriage, but you've proved that you're ready to begin the journey. Satisfied with your knowledge, the preacher smiles. He's now ready to lead you in the vows that will enjoin your destinies and officially send you on your journey toward the deepest levels of intimacy. But before your lips may come together in the wedding kiss, your minds must be forever entwined, not as a single, robotic unit of constantly friction-free agreement, but as independent entities, promising to always work together for the good of the relationship instead of an individual agenda.

"Are you ready to be united with one another, to become a unit of 'We,' instead of merely a 'Me'?" the preacher asks. "I know from what you've told me that you realize that the word *we* means you're a team, a permanent combination of who you both are into a sharing of what's best for both of you. Now that you are embarking upon this journey toward intimacy, you must no longer demand your own way, but a way that is best for the both of you. Everything you do from this moment forward will dramatically affect the other. Are you ready to proceed?"

You nod your heads in simultaneous agreement, and the preacher continues.

> Please repeat these vows after me, and, in the spirit of future communication between the two of you, do not merely let them linger on your lips. Do not repeat these vows and then forget them, but instead allow them to permeate your being and your life. For these are the laws that you must live by; their denial, neglect, or invalidation will immediately send you back to where you began, and you will have to start the journey all over again, perhaps even alone.

And then the preacher begins reciting your vows.

"When there are differences and conflicts between you, which are normal, do you promise to take turns and carefully listen to each other?" he asks.

You smile at each other and say in unison, "We do."

"Do you promise to set your own opinions, concerns, and expectations aside during your conversations and do all that you can to understand what your mate is saying and understand who he or she is as a person?"

"We do," you say.

"Do you promise to accept and value your mate's uniqueness as separate from you but also special and treasured?" he asks.

"We do," you reply.

"Do you promise to strive for mutual agreement in all of your solutions to the conflicts you will encounter together, thereby blending yourselves together in unity?"

"We do," you promise.

"Do you promise to discover your mate's deepest relational needs and do all that you can to meet those needs, or instead to lead your mate to the sources that will meet their deepest needs?"

"We do," you say. Now comes the most important vow, one comprising the three basic skills that will deliver you to the deepest levels of intimacy.

"Do you promise to honor, communicate, and recharge each other with love until death do you part?" he asks.

"We solemnly swear, we do," you say.

The preacher's voice rises.

Guard your union above all earthly things. Lay down your emotional armor and fight for your relationship every day. Knock down the boundaries between you, remove the walls, and open your minds and hearts completely to each other without exception. Once you do that, you will be ready to begin the journey to the deepest depths of intimacy. You are now equipped for that journey, a pilgrimage that doesn't happen once and end in deliverance, but instead must be taken over and over again, each day of your years together. The secret of optimum relationships is the eternal willingness to face the struggle, the admission that "We're in this together." You must learn to face differences, pain, resistance, and, most of all, fear *together*, putting your relationship on high and, in doing so, promising yourselves that you will not succumb to the cycle of conflict, division, and decay. Commit yourself to the day-to-day work that optimum relationships require. And always remember that the moment you decide you've achieved the deepest level of intimacy and there is no more work to be done, you will be sentenced to return to the superficial levels you have worked so hard to move beyond.

You nod your heads in agreement, then exchange rings, all the while staring into each other's eyes.

"As you have solemnly vowed before God and these witnesses, and with the authority invested in me by the state, I now pronounce you lawfully married, husband and wife. You may kiss the bride!"

You embrace for the wedding kiss, and the congregation explodes in applause and congratulations.

The preacher directs his attention to the congregation.

"It's my privilege to congratulate and introduce you to . . ."

And he shouts your names in exaltation, no longer separate but now a cohesive unit, the "Mr. and Mrs." of eternal dedication, honor, and love. You march down the aisle into the journey of your lifetime, the journey toward real and lasting intimacy.

The time has arrived for you to go forth in a new beginning. Take a deep breath and your mate by the hand, and then dive into the waters of intimacy. Dive deep and long toward the limits of your mind, body, and soul. The initial shock may be bracing, even scary, but once you reach the depths, a new world will open itself to you. It's the world proclaimed in poetry and song, a place of which everyone dreams but few truly experience, a world that can be as elusive as a faraway planet, even when it's twinkling right over your shoulder: the deepest recesses of the human heart.

May you delve deeply into this wondrous world, embrace it, and revel in its glories. Then, and only then, will you experience life's greatest gift: to love and be loved in return.

ABOUT THE AUTHOR

GARY SMALLEY is one of the country's best-known authors and speakers on family relationships. He is the author or coauthor of sixteen best-selling, award-winning books along with several popular films and videos. He has spent over thirty years learning, teaching, and counseling. Gary has personally interviewed hundreds of singles and couples, and has surveyed thousands of people at his seminars, asking two questions: What is it that strengthens your relationships? And what weakens them?

Gary received his bachelor's degree in psychology from Long Beach State University in California. He has a master's degree and has received two honorary doctorate degrees in educational counseling and psychology for his thirty years of research.

Gary's books combined have sold close to 4 million copies. Several of them have been translated into several different languages. *The Blessing* and *The Two Sides of Love* have won the Golden Medallion Award for excellence in literature. *The Language of Love* won the Angel Award as the best contribution to family life. All the other titles have been top-five finalists for the Gold Medallion Award.

In the past ten years, Gary has spoken to more than 1 million people. His national infomercial *Hidden Keys to Loving Relationships* has appeared to television audiences all over the world. The eighteen-videotape series of the same name has sold more than 4 million copies.

Gary and his wife, Norma, have been married for thirty-five years and live in Branson, Missouri. They have three children—Kari Gibson, a children's author; Dr. Greg Smalley; and Michael Smalley, a Ph.D. candidate in psychology—and six grandchildren.

Gary Smalley's speaking schedule and video products can be found at www.garysmalley.com.